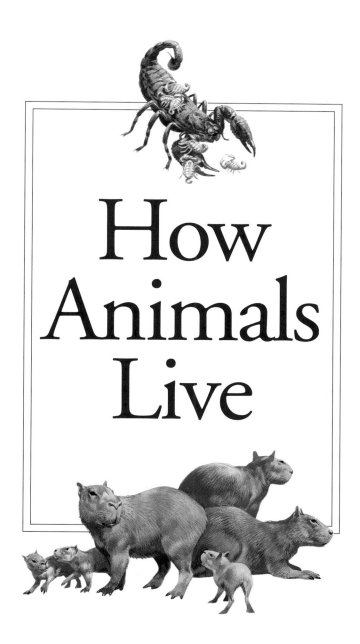

How
Animals
Live

Library of Congress Cataloging-in-Publication Data available

0-439-54834-9

10 9 8 7 6 5 4 3 2 1   04 05 06
07 08

Printed in Dubai, UAE
First printing, March 2004

Bernard Stonehouse
and Esther Bertram

How
Animals
Live

THE AMAZING WORLD OF ANIMALS
IN THE WILD

ILLUSTRATED BY

John Francis

SCHOLASTIC
REFERENCE

FOR VIV

FOR FIRECREST

Art and Editorial Direction by
Peter Sackett

Editor
Norman Barrett

Designer
Paul Richards, Designers & Partners

Color separation by
SC (Sang Choy) International Pte Ltd

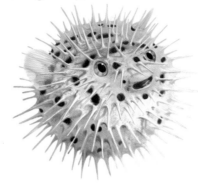

FOR SCHOLASTIC

Editorial Director	**Kenneth Wright**
Editors	**Virginia Ann Koeth** **Danielle Denega**
Managing Editor	**Manuela Soares**
Production Editor	**Karen Capria**
Copy Editor	**Martin Walsh**
Art Director	**Nancy Sabato**
Designer	**Kristina Albertson**

Introduction

Anyone who is interested in living creatures — and that means most of us — watches animals and plants from time to time, and marvels at the hundreds of different ways in which they live. Before long come the questions, to which there is virtually no end. How do birds build their nests? Why do they build different kinds of nests? Why are some animals brightly colored and others drab? Why do some show off, while others live in hiding? Why are some fierce and others gentle? Do crocodiles eat their young? Do bears talk to each other? How can a fish live inside a jellyfish? Do cats see what we see? How do owls hunt in the dark? How do mice keep out of their way? Why are some animals poisonous?

Scientists who are interested in how animals live may spend their lifetimes studying animal behaviors. They watch animals in the wild, in jungles and deserts, among snow and ice, up in the mountains, or down in the oceans, trying to answer these questions and others like them. The more scientists learn, the more they are impressed by the ways animals survive in an unfriendly world.

This book is about what animals do to keep themselves alive, and how they live as comfortably and efficiently as possible. It covers a wide range of animals, mostly birds and mammals, but reptiles, amphibians, fish, insects, and others, too. Some are familiar, everyday kinds of animals. Others are strange and exotic, and you would be lucky to see them even in zoos. This is not only a book for children — it is for anyone who is interested in animals and their behaviors.

BERNARD STONEHOUSE
ESTHER BERTRAM

Contents

CHAPTER 1

Starting Out in Life

We are used to human babies that look very much like ourselves, only smaller. Human infants take a lot of caring for, especially during their first few years, when there is little they can do for themselves. They still need care as they grow, when they are learning the ways of the world. That is what families are about – the young learn from adults, often mothers, fathers, grandparents, uncles, aunts, and older brothers and sisters, who protect them from dangers and show them how to live. They also learn from children of similar age in their neighborhood.

This is all very different from the way most animals start out in life and grow. Many kinds of animals never see their parents, brothers, or sisters, and have no family life. No other mammals – the group of warm-blooded animals to which humans belong – have so long a childhood. They seldom have time – some of the smaller mammals, such as mice and rabbits, become parents themselves within a few weeks of birth. Simpler animals, such as insects and earthworms, could not learn from the examples of others – their brains do not work that way. This chapter discusses different animals that start life in different ways.

Insects and other invertebrates go through several stages to become adults. Fish, amphibians, and reptiles usually hatch from eggs and grow up on their own. Birds, too, hatch from eggs, but both the eggs and the nestlings receive parental care. It is mostly young mammals that enjoy long-term help from one or both parents, some of them for weeks, months, or even years.

Young Canadian beavers enjoy the comfort and safety of dry sleeping areas in "lodges" that their parents build. The cubs stay with their parents for at least two years, learning how to survive.

Surinam Toad

When a female Surinam toad is ready to lay eggs, she finds a mate who grabs her and holds her tightly. Together, they swim in circles like a Ferris wheel. At the top of each turn she produces six eggs, which the male presses into pits in the soft spongy skin of her back. Over the next four weeks, each egg develops safely in its own pit.

The male presses the eggs into the soft skin on the female's back.

(1) Each egg develops into a tiny tadpole. (2) The tadpole grows inside the egg. (3) The tadpole turns into a tiny toad and (4) breaks out, ready to swim off.

1

2

3

4

As soon as they break free from their eggs, the tiny toads are off. They are good enough swimmers to avoid the many predators that lurk in the muddy streams where they live.

Platypus

Most mammals give birth to live young. This platypus is a very unusual Australian mammal that lays eggs and incubates them like a bird. The eggs are hidden away inside a burrow in a stream bank. The platypus keeps them warm, curling round them and holding them under her tail until they hatch. She feeds the young milk, and they stay with her for a few weeks, learning how to live safely in a dangerous world.

• Strange Beginnings •
Protecting the eggs

American Alligator

This female American alligator, about 10 feet (3 m) long, has laid 20 eggs in a scraped-up pile of sand, and hidden them under a pile of rotting grass and reeds. She will stay close, but does not need to keep them warm. They are warm enough to develop slowly without

her. In five or six weeks, 16 to 20 little alligators, each about 8 inches (20 cm) long, will emerge from the nest. She will hear them squeaking, and may help some of them to break out of their eggs. Then they will go their separate ways.

The mother may help her babies out, even holding eggs in her mouth to crack the tough shells.

Many animals need special protection before birth – when they are inside the egg. Some mothers have unusual ways of looking after their eggs, making sure that they have every chance of hatching safely.

The Surinam toad (opposite page) lives in crowded streams and rivers, full of predators that would eat eggs and tiny tadpoles if they had the chance. So the mother toad keeps her eggs and tadpoles with her, carrying them on her back until they turn into toads. Then they can swim strongly enough to escape.

Seahorses also carry their eggs with them

The female passes the eggs into her mate's pouch (above right). The baby seahorses swim out from their father's pouch (above).

for safety. In this case the males take charge, carrying them in pouches on their stomachs. Fish usually lay eggs and leave them to develop among rocks and seaweed on the seabed. Mother alligators protect their eggs by hiding them in nests under mounds of rotting vegetation. Platypus mothers do the same. The vegetation keeps the eggs out of harm's way, and helps to incubate them at the same time. A crustacean called the triops lays eggs that might have to survive in dry mud for several years before they can hatch.

Seahorse

Here (right) is a seahorse with a belly full of eggs. It is a male seahorse, not a female. His mate laid the eggs into a pouch on his belly, which is safer than laying them on the seabed. He will carry them around for four to five weeks, the time it takes for them to develop into tiny seahorses. When they are ready, they will leave the pouch and swim off to the safety of a seaweed bed.

The male with a pouch full of eggs.

Triops

Triops (the name means three-eyed) are crustaceans about 1 inch (2.5 cm) long. These particular ones live in a shallow pond in the very dry Mojave Desert of southern California. It is summer, and soon the pond will dry up – it may not rain again for 20 years. So what will happen to the triops? These will all die, but not before laying tough-shelled eggs that will survive year after year in the dry mud. As soon as it rains, the eggs will hatch, and there will be more triops.

The tiny eggs survive in the dry mud.

· Strange Beginnings ·

Growing up different

Even at one week old, a human baby is recognizable as human. But most animals produce young that look different from themselves. Usually these young live in different places from their parents and feed on different foods, avoiding both competition with their parents and the dangers of their world. These creatures take on different shapes and forms as they grow to maturity. This caterpillar (main picture, opposite page) – called a "woolly bear" because of its covering of prickly fur – is the baby of the garden tiger moth, a

species quite common in both Europe and the United States. The prickles and a poison in its skin make it bad news for any bird that tries to eat it. Male and female moths find each other by scent, and the females lay tiny eggs on the leaves of a wide range of shrubs. Hatching a few days later, the caterpillars never see or know their parents.

Puss-Moth

This "monster" (below) is the caterpillar, or larva, of a puss-moth (further below). About two months old and already 2 inches (5 cm) long, it has lived apart from its parents, taking care of itself from the moment it hatched from a tiny egg.

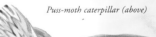

Puss-moth caterpillar (above)

Adult puss-moth (above)

Adult puss-moths are silver-gray and covered with soft, silky fur. When the caterpillar is mature, it finds a crack in a tree, weaves a silky jacket, or cocoon, and turns into a chrysalis. Inside the chrysalis during winter it changes into an adult, emerging in spring.

Common Jellyfish

Jellyfish are found in all oceans. The biggest grow to more than 6 feet (2 m) across, with tentacles five or six times as long. Adults produce eggs, often hundreds at a time, that hatch into microscopic larvae. These float in surface waters, then sink to the seabed. They attach themselves face-up to weeds or rocks, and turn into something that looks like a tiny sea anemone. This starts budding off another kind of larva that looks like an eight-petalled flower. These larvae float free, return to the sea surface, and eventually grow into adult jellyfish.

Free-floating and beautiful, the common jellyfish feeds on fish, shrimps, and other small animals that it catches in its tentacles.

Cranefly

Here is a cranefly, an insect about 1 inch (2.5 cm) long, with a single pair of long, thin wings and six long, spindly legs. Why "cranefly"? Because it reminds people of long-legged birds called cranes. Craneflies emerge in swarms around late spring and summer, often flying into houses and dancing on the windows. They lay batches of eggs in the soil, and take no further care of them. Each egg develops into a small grub called a leather-jacket, which eats grass roots. The one pictured (inset above) is already a year old and fully grown – also about 1 inch long. It will soon become inactive, grow a hard case around itself, and turn into a pupa. After a few weeks, the pupa will split, and from it will emerge (inset below) something quite different – a cranefly.

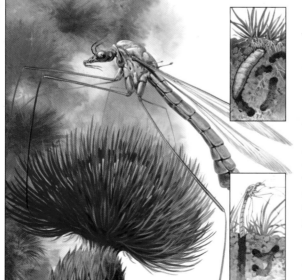

Garden Tiger Moth

Woolly bear caterpillars, tiny at first, munch the leaves on which they hatch. Growing quickly, they move on to find other leaves. Sometimes thousands hatch and grow together, eating all the leaves off hundreds of shrubs, even crossing roads in search of more food. Then each caterpillar turns into a pupa, or chrysalis, emerging as an adult moth (see page 69) in the spring.

These tiny caterpillars grow quickly by eating all the leaves of nearby bushes.

American Bullfrog

The creature with a long tail and legs (below) is a tadpole – the larva, or young form, of a frog. It lives in a stream in the southeastern United States. In a few weeks, it will turn into a small American bullfrog, with a green and yellow coat. In about four years it will have grown into an adult bullfrog – (left) up to 6 inches (15 cm) long.

Common Lobster

This female lobster's dark, green-blue shell matches her underwater environment well. She has produced several dozen small, translucent eggs, which she carries for a few days on her body. The eggs will ripen, detach themselves, and float off, rising to the sea surface. There they will hatch into tiny, transparent larvae, which drift with currents and tides. Feeding on even tinier plant cells, and later small floating animals, the larvae will grow, passing through several crab-like stages to reach the large-eyed form (below) that begins to resemble its parents.

The maturing lobster develops much bigger claws and a stronger body.

Naked Mole Rat

These toothy, rat-like mammals, found in the hot deserts of northeast Africa, live underground in deep chambers to avoid predators. Almost bald, they live in crowded colonies, feeding on roots and bulbs. Only a few individuals grow as big as their parents, come to the surface, and produce offspring. The rest remain small – underground workers that never breed.

• Strange Beginnings •

Weird creatures

Most young animals begin life looking different from their parents, and some look quite extraordinary, even weird. This young lobster (main picture) is beginning to look more like its parents, but those large, bulging eyes give it an almost frightening appearance. It has been living as a larva at the sea surface, and is now sinking down to the seabed, where it will spend the rest of its life. In the dim light among seaweeds 100 feet (30 m) down, it will be hard to see, and those legs and antennae will look like strands of weed. It will find a home in a hole, emerging only to look for food.

Dragonfly nymphs, stocky and squat, are very different from their beautiful, delicate parents. Young mole rats living underground in the hot African desert do look like their parents – their skin almost bare, with just a few long, sensitive hairs, and they have only tiny eyes and ears. Larval goose barnacles, like larval lobsters, feed at the sea surface before settling as adults. Young hoatzins have wing claws that help them to grip and climb among the branches.

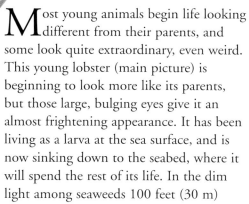

Goose Barnacle

A larval goose barnacle (bottom right picture) is tiny, less than 0.1 inch (2.5 mm) long. Seen under a microscope, these animals have transparent shells, beady eyes, and lots of legs. They are crustaceans, related to lobsters, and live at the sea surface. Adult goose barnacles (above), 2–3 inches (5–7.5 cm) long, live in clusters on logs and on seaweed floating on the sea surface. When the time comes, the barnacle releases eggs from its shell into the water. The eggs hatch into the tiny larvae.

Inside the shell (left) the barnacle looks like a tiny shrimp.

Hoatzin

This young hoatzin lives in the Amazon rainforest, feeding on leaves and fruit. Though a bird, it has weak wing muscles and cannot fly well. Instead, it searches for food by scrambling among the tree branches around its nest, using its wings like hands. The claw on the front of its wing is a thumbnail that helps it to hang on. Later in life this will disappear.

Young hoatzins can swim well.

The adult dragonfly emerges from the back of the nymph.

Dragonfly

Beautiful insects with two pairs of transparent wings, dragonflies look nothing like their larva, shown attacking a tadpole (far left). They lay eggs on reeds close to streams or ponds. The eggs hatch into these strange larvae, or nymphs, which spend a year or more foraging on the muddy bottom before turning into flying adults.

Imperial dragonflies spend months as nymphs, but only a few days as flying adults (left).

20161773

Dor Beetle

This adult dor, or dung, beetle uses its feet to roll balls of antelope dung to soft ground, where it will dig a hole 2–3 inches (5–7.5 cm) deep. It pushes two or three balls into the hole, one containing an egg. Without further help from the parent, the egg hatches, and the larva feeds on the dung, pupates, and develops into a beetle.

Common Snail

Snails breed by laying packages of 40 to 50 fertile eggs a few inches down in the soil (1). After about seven weeks, the eggs hatch into tiny snails with soft, transparent shells (2). These feed by grazing algae and other living organisms from the soil. The shells quickly become chalky and harden. As the soft-bodied snails grow (3), they add rings to the lip of the shell, so it is always large enough for them to retreat into it.

• Growing up Alone •

Born alone

Young humans cannot look after themselves. Mothers and other members of the family help in rearing them. In the animal world, most mothers lay eggs, rather than produce live young, and most eggs are left to hatch on their own. So the young never see their parents. From the moment of hatching, the larvae or young forms need to be able to survive alone.

This common snail (main picture) has laid its eggs in the soil and will leave them to fend for themselves. The young snails will hatch and immediately start to feed on what is closest to them – green plant cells and other small creatures in the soil.

Dogfish produce small groups of eggs that attach themselves to weeds on the sea floor and hatch alone. Each contains a larva or embryo with a store of food that helps the young to survive for the first few days of life. Caddis flies lay eggs that hatch into larvae and are soon feeding and protecting themselves. Young dor beetles hatch alone in a ball of dung that the adult has hidden underground. Horseshoe crab larvae emerge in the hundreds from eggs that hatch long after their parents have moved on.

The dor beetle larva (which looks like a hairy caterpillar) grows and eventually changes into a pupa, from which emerges an adult flying beetle (above).

Caddis Fly

You find caddis fly larvae under stones in freshwater streams throughout spring and summer. Adult caddis flies lay their eggs in tiny clusters on the surface of the water. The eggs sink and hatch into larvae, which secrete a papery case around themselves, and then stick grains of sand and tiny pebbles to the case to strengthen it. They feed by trapping small plants and animals.

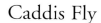

1

2

3

Different species of larvae make their cases from different materials: (1) sand and grit, (2) snail shells, (3) twigs.

After a few months to a year, the larvae pupate and turn into adult flies (left).

Dogfish

Dogfish are small sharks, 4 feet (1.2 m) long – named for the way they hunt in packs like dogs. Lesser spotted dogfish produce large eggs, packed in a shell with yolk for the growing embryo to feed on. Each egg is inside a case. The young emerge to feed and fend for themselves, leaving the familiar case or "mermaid's purse" (left) behind.

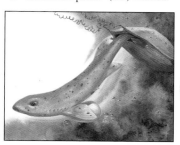

Atlantic Horseshoe Crab

Atlantic horseshoe crabs, up to 2 feet (60 cm) long (right), live along the coast of North America. When breeding, thousands gather in the shallows, and at high tide the females dig pits in the sand, laying about 1,000 eggs, which the males fertilize. When the eggs hatch, the larvae first feed at the surface, then sink to the seabed and grow in stages to adult size over nine years.

Young crab

First hatching

Breaking out alone

Here are more animals whose young have to look after themselves right from the start. The black-spotted, slithery red creature on the opposite page is a salamander, an amphibian. Though it looks like a lizard, it is more closely related to the frog. It has a soft, moist skin and needs to live in a damp place close to water. Adult red salamanders mate on damp ground at the edges of ponds and streams, and the females lay their eggs in small batches close by. On hatching, the larval salamanders break out without help from their parents, and wriggle into the

water. Though the adults can live on land, the larvae are like tadpoles, and catch their food in the water. Each larva hatches with a small supply of food in a yolk sac, which helps it to survive alone until it can catch its own food. Salamanders' brains are strong on instincts, or built-in behavior, but weak on learning. Even if the parents stayed close, the young salamanders are so different, with a different way of life, that they would not be able to learn much from them. This is true, too, for the other animals on this page, all reptiles.

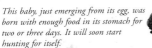

This baby, just emerging from its egg, was born with enough food in its stomach for two or three days. It will soon start hunting for itself.

Gila Monster

Gila monsters, 2 feet (60 cm) long, are lizards that live in the southwestern United States. Called monsters because of their poisonous bite, they kill insects, small mammals, and birds with an injection of poison from their lower jaw.

Scarlet King Snake

This scarlet king snake, like most other snakes, breaks out of its egg alone. King snakes are constrictors, or squeezers. This one will soon discover that it can catch and squeeze other small animals to death, and swallow them whole.

Eastern Box Turtle

Turtles are tortoises that live in or very near water. Eastern box turtles live in the southeastern corner of the United States, on damp, marshy ground. They grow to about 6 inches (15 cm) long. After mating, the females lay 20 or more eggs in holes in the ground, which they cover and leave. A few weeks later, the little turtles use a spike or "egg tooth" on their nose to break out of the egg, and scramble up to the surface. Within hours of hatching they are feeding and fending for themselves.

The eggs laid in damp sand hatch without any help from parents.

Box turtles have hinges on the underside of their shells. When threatened by a predator, they close the shell like a box.

The larva has enough food to enable it to survive for a few days.

Feathery gills help the larva breathe until its lungs develop.

Red salamanders lay their eggs close to water.

Red Salamander

In daytime, salamanders as bright as this one would be easy prey. So they come out mainly at night, into a cool, watery world where they hunt for tiny insects and slugs, finding them mainly by scent. They lay their eggs near water. The eggs hatch to produce tadpole-like larvae which carry their own food supply, enough for a few days, until they figure out how to catch tiny particles of food for themselves.

Rattlesnake

Snakes generally make very little sound – just a quiet "hiss-ss-ss" when disturbed. But adult rattlesnakes have a rattle and young ones grow them in their second or third year. As rattlesnakes grow, they shed their skin two or three times a year, and the rattle builds up from segments of dried tail skin. It is thought they use the rattle as a warning, reminding big mammals not to tread accidentally on them.

The rattle (at the end of the tail) grows larger each time the snake sheds its skin.

• Growing up Alone •
Surviving alone

Black-Headed Duck

Black-headed ducks of South America lay their eggs singly in the nests of other, usually smaller, ducks. The chicks are reared by these foster parents. But they instinctively know how to dive and catch their food underwater.

The black-headed duckling (above right) is larger than its foster brothers and sisters, and wins out when it comes to feeding.

Human mothers feed their babies on milk from their own breasts, or milk glands. So do other mammals, such as cows, rabbits, and guinea pigs. While the young are being cared for, they have time to learn many other things about life from their parents. They have the kinds of brains that allow them to learn. Most other kinds of animals do not have "learning" brains. Even if they had, their lives are short, and they would not have time for useful learning. Instead they have instincts – built-in knowledge that comes into play soon after they are born and helps them to survive on their own.

Rattlesnakes produce eggs, but keep them inside their bodies until they hatch, so the

young are born alive. The one opposite was born just over an hour ago, together with a dozen more brothers and sisters. Their mother slid off as soon as they appeared. They won't see her again. But, equipped with poison fangs, they will soon start catching lizards, mice, and other small prey. As well as reptiles like the rattlesnake, fish, insects, and birds also hatch from eggs and have to use their instincts to survive; these include the salmon, ant lion, and, with the help of foster parents, the cuckoo and the black-headed duck.

Cuckoo

Cuckoos build no nests, instead laying their eggs in the nests of other birds. The cuckoo's egg matches those of the hosts, but is usually larger and hatches more quickly. The hatchling cuckoo throws the remaining eggs from the nest, so the foster parents have only one mouth – a very large one – to feed.

Having heaved all the other eggs from the nest, the young cuckoo receives all the food that its foster parents can bring. Within three or four weeks it may grow to twice the size of its hosts, who continue to feed it until it finally flies away.

Ant Lion (Doodlebug)

The ant lion, or doodlebug, (below) is the larva of a fly. After hatching, it dug itself a pit about an inch deep in firm sand, and sat there waiting for ants and other small prey to fall in. It injects them with poison, and sucks out their juices.

The larval ant lion, after turning into a pupa, or resting stage, emerges in adult form as a lacey-winged fly (right).

Atlantic Salmon

Salmon begin life as jelly-covered eggs laid in gravel in a mountain stream. The parents leave the eggs soon after laying them (below). After hatching, the tiny larval salmon drift downstream, feeding first on their own yolks, then on algae and tiny insect larvae in the water. When about half grown, they

head toward the ocean, fattening as they go. As adults they will return to the river where they were hatched, fighting their way upstream like this big male (right), to mate and produce eggs of their own.

Giant Anteater

Ants and termites are plentiful, particularly in warm countries, and several different kinds of mammals specialize in eating·them. There is not much nourishment in a single ant, but an ants' nest may hold millions of them, plus eggs and grubs. Anteaters rear one baby at a time, so each youngster receives plenty of care and attention from its mother. Carrying it on her back until it is well over half-grown, she gives it many opportunities to figure out how to live and catch ants for itself.

Anteaters raise and carry only one young at a time. During the rainy season, the anteater swims its precious cargo to the safety of high ground.

• Parental Care •

In safe keeping

Japanese Macaque

Japanese macaques are a kind of monkey that lives only in Japan. Adults reach 18–24 inches (45–60 cm). Short-tailed, with pink faces, they band together, sometimes in troops of 100 or more, especially where food is plentiful. Males and females seldom stay together long after mating, but the infants are brought up within family groups, fed and carried by their own mothers. When a predator threatens, the whole troop gathers around, shouting, screaming, and leaping up and down to drive the danger away.

The young anteater on its mother's back (opposite) lives on the dry plains of South America. Just a few weeks old, and still small, it depends for its life on the protection of grown-ups, particularly on its mother's care and skills. It grows slowly but steadily – after about a year it will be as big as its mother, and too big to be carried. Meanwhile, it watches as she tears open an ants' nest, then starts to lick up the ants. The mother does not set out to teach, but the young anteater learns – just by being there and seeing what she does.

Before long it will itself be tearing at ants' nests and licking up the ants. Then it will go off on its own.

Young dolphins in the sea and macaques in the forest are protected from danger by groups of adults that encircle them and keep them safe from predators and other danger. Rhinoceroses and koalas, being more solitary creatures, protect their young alone. The young watch and learn how their parents cope with life, until finally they can fend for themselves.

Bottlenose Dolphin

Named for their bottle-shaped noses, these dolphins live in temperate waters of the North Atlantic Ocean and Mediterranean Sea, growing to 12 feet (3.6 m) long. A newborn born calf, only a little over 3 feet (1 m) long, swims as soon as it is born, staying close to its mother, and feeding from time to time on her rich milk. Small dolphins are often in danger from sharks and other predatory fish. Dolphins swim protectively around their calves, ready to fend off sharks by jabbing fiercely with their long noses.

A dolphin bumps a shark with its nose.

Black Rhinoceros

African black rhinos stand up to 5 feet (1.5 m) tall and weigh as much as small trucks. This calf, only 30 inches (75 cm) high, is smaller than the spotted hyena that threatens it. The calf stays close to its mother, turning when she turns. Hyenas know better than to come within reach of that huge horn.

Both young koalas and young rhinos stick close to their mothers, learning from them when danger threatens, where to find food, and what is good to eat.

Koala

Koalas are marsupial mammals that live in northeastern Australia. Marsupials give birth to very tiny babies, keeping them in a pouch permanently attached to the milk glands. Only 1 inch (2.5 cm) long, newborn koalas are just strong enough to crawl into the pouch. They grow slowly, and after a few months are big enough to leave the pouch and be carried on the mother's back.

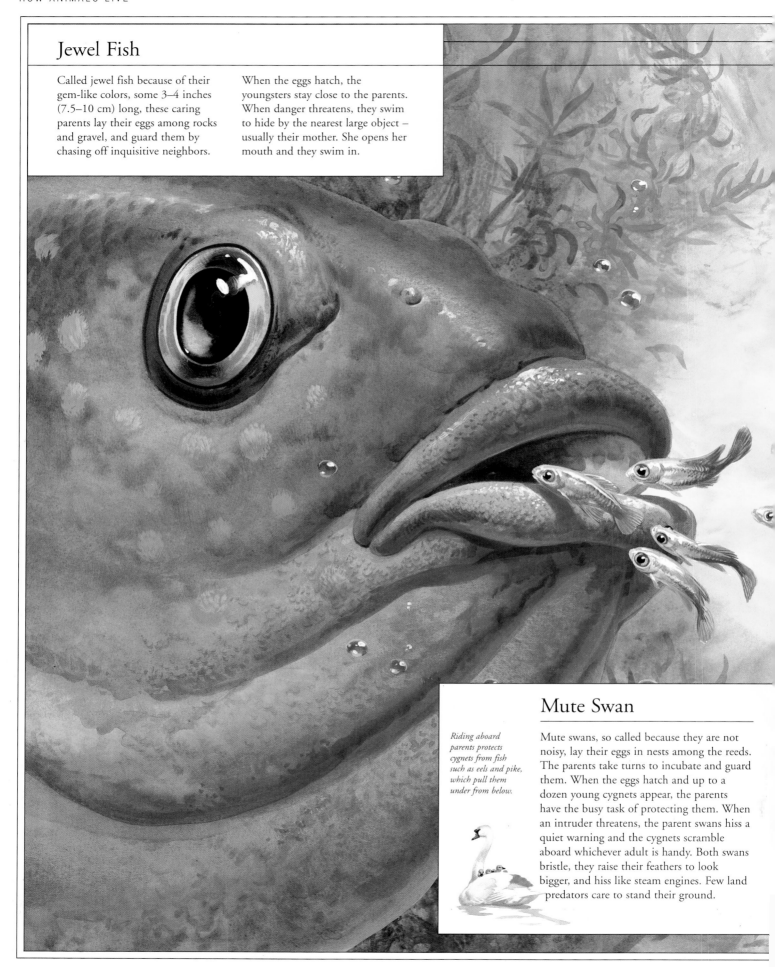

Jewel Fish

Called jewel fish because of their gem-like colors, some 3–4 inches (7.5–10 cm) long, these caring parents lay their eggs among rocks and gravel, and guard them by chasing off inquisitive neighbors.

When the eggs hatch, the youngsters stay close to the parents. When danger threatens, they swim to hide by the nearest large object – usually their mother. She opens her mouth and they swim in.

Mute Swan

Riding aboard parents protects cygnets from fish such as eels and pike, which pull them under from below.

Mute swans, so called because they are not noisy, lay their eggs in nests among the reeds. The parents take turns to incubate and guard them. When the eggs hatch and up to a dozen young cygnets appear, the parents have the busy task of protecting them. When an intruder threatens, the parent swans hiss a quiet warning and the cygnets scramble aboard whichever adult is handy. Both swans bristle, they raise their feathers to look bigger, and hiss like steam engines. Few land predators care to stand their ground.

• Parental Care •
Full-time caring

Woolly Opossum

These South American marsupials give birth to tiny young, which they keep in a pouch. When the young outgrow the pouch, they cling to their mother's stomach as she forages in the trees for leaves and fruit (see also pages 28-29).

The hatchlings swim into their mother's mouth for safety..

In facing the dangers of everyday life, adult animals generally stand a better chance than their offspring. Smaller than their parents and less experienced in the ways of the world, young animals are far more at risk. For mammals, birds, and other animals that spend time with their young, caring can be a dangerous job. A parent has both itself and its young ones to feed when food is scarce, and to protect when there are predators about.

Different animals have different ways of keeping their young from harm. The female jewel fish (opposite page) protects her larvae by opening her mouth and letting them hide inside. How do the larvae know that this is safe? They don't – they would be just as likely to hide in a hole in the rocks, but she is nearer. Swans and scorpions let their youngsters ride on their backs, keeping them from dangerous predators. Baby opossums cling to their mother's stomach up in the trees, while leopardesses constantly change the dens or hiding places where they keep their cubs, so that predators do not find them.

Leopard

Leopards are members of the cat family that hunt on the African plains. Females produce and raise their cubs alone. At five weeks old, though big enough to walk and scramble about, they are still too small to defend themselves against predatory snakes, hunting dogs, jackals, and hyenas. Sleeping most of the day in the den, the cubs wait for their mother to return from hunting. The den becomes smelly, and may attract predators that hunt by scent. So every few days the mother moves the cubs one by one to a clean, new den.

Leopard cubs have much to learn – this one is trying to catch a frog.

Imperial Scorpion

Scorpions live mostly in dry, tropical countries, the largest growing to 8 inches (20 cm) long. Eight-legged, they have large pincers, which they use in fighting. The sting carried in the tail has been known to kill humans. Hunting mainly at night, they attack beetles and spiders, tearing them to pieces. Females may even attack and kill males with which they have recently mated. Rather surprisingly, those same female scorpions are caring mothers that carry newborn young on their backs until they are old enough to fend for themselves.

Mother scorpions carry their young on their backs for several weeks.

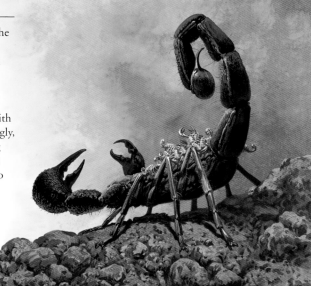

• Parental Care •

House dad

Human mothers generally take most responsibility for bringing up the children, and so do those of most animals that show parental care. In just a few animals, males are the major caregivers – "house dads" with different methods for incubating and protecting the young. This male emperor penguin (main picture) is one of several thousand forming a colony on Antarctica. Through the coldest weeks of winter he incubates his egg for over 60 days, holding it on his feet to keep it warm. His partner spends the time several miles away at sea, fattening and preparing to return to feed the newly hatched chick.

Female seahorses lay the eggs, but males carry them around in a belly pouch until they hatch (see page 11). Another male fish, the stickleback, guards the eggs and then the hatchlings. Among the flightless kiwis and cassowaries, only the males incubate eggs. Mallee fowl males build enormous compost heaps to keep the eggs at the right temperature for incubation.

Cassowary

The male cassowary, as tall as a man, lives in the rainforests of Australia and New Guinea. After mating with a female, he incubates the eggs and cares for the chicks alone, defending them fiercely with razor-sharp nails on his feet.

Stickleback

Several species of these small, silvery-blue fish are common in ponds and streams. Males of some species build tunnel nests of small twigs and attract the females in to lay. The males fertilize the eggs, then

guard them carefully, fanning streams of water over them to keep them supplied with oxygen. Later, they tend to the hatchlings, too.

Kiwi

Kiwis, distantly related to ostriches but much smaller, stand about 16 inches (40 cm) tall. They live in New Zealand. They come out only at night and are seldom seen. Hens lay one big egg, usually in a cave or hollow. Only the males – which are smaller than the females – incubate the egg, for about 10 weeks. When the chick hatches, it stays in the nest for four or five days without feeding, then leaves to feed alone.

Kiwis usually lay one very large egg, which the male alone incubates.

Mallee Fowl

This male mallee fowl of Australia is digging a pit to fill with leaves for a huge nest. When it is warm enough, he lets his mate lay her eggs in it, and stands guard. He tests the temperature from time to time with his bill, opening the heap to adjust the temperature until the chicks emerge.

Emperor Penguin

Emperor penguins, the largest penguins, stand up to 45 inches (115 cm) tall. In autumn they gather on the newly formed sea ice around Antarctica to mate and lay their single eggs. Then the females leave for the sea, while the males incubate the eggs on their feet. At hatching, the females return, and the two parents alternate watching their young. Later both parents leave to bring food back.

This grown chick is almost ready to go to sea.

Emperor chicks huddle together to keep warm while both parents forage for food at sea.

Polar Bear

Polar bears live in the cold Arctic. In autumn the pregnant female digs a cave in a snowdrift and lets herself be sealed in. The young are born and reared throughout winter. In spring the mother and cubs leave the cave in search of food.

Woolly Opossum

Here is a family of woolly opossums in South America. Like their cousins in Australia, the females keep their five or six new-born young in a small pouch – to protect them against the dangers of the forest. When the young grow too big to fit in, they cling to the mother as she forages in the trees. Some of these youngsters still hitch rides, although they are old enough now to cling by their tails to the branches (see also page 25).

These young woolly opossums are learning how to survive alone in the tropical forests. For now their mother is in charge, ready to protect them with her pin-sharp teeth.

The family

Human families usually include two parents, children, plus cousins, aunts, uncles, and grandparents. The same is true for many other kinds of mammals and for some birds that live in family groups. Generally the mother takes the main responsibility for the youngsters (but see House dads; pp. 26–7), while the rest of the group give other kinds of support. These young woolly opossums look quite a handful for their mother. They will stay together as a family until they are able to survive on their own. Young polar bears depend on their mothers for two or more years, learning how to hunt in harsh conditions, but gaining no support from fathers or other kin. It is also the mother woolly opossum who looks after her babies. Rabbits live in large family groups of several mothers with their young, in warrens that extend below the ground. Beavers build up large family groups, in which all the members keep busy building and maintaining their lodges and dams.

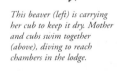

Polar bear cubs stay with their mother for two years or more as they learn about survival in cold Arctic lands.

Canadian Beaver

Families of Canadian beavers live in "lodges" made from felled trees. These include dams which they build across the river. Young beavers stay with their parents for two years, living in the lodges, gnawing young trees, and dragging or floating them to the lodge to help with the constant maintenance.

This beaver (left) is carrying her cub to keep it dry. Mother and cubs swim together (above), diving to reach chambers in the lodge.

Rabbit

After about two weeks the young rabbits surface for the first time. Still the doe stays with them, marking them with her own scent from a grease gland under her chin.

Rabbit warrens, or burrows, are good defense against predators from the air, but the doe (female) stands little chance against land invaders such as stoats and weasels. Big warrens with several hundred burrows are home to many does, each with her own nesting chamber. Does gives birth to between three and eight babies, which feed on her milk (below). After about five weeks they leave the burrow for good, and some seven weeks later may themselves be parents.

Prairie Dog

Prairie dogs are squirrel-like rodents, closely akin to rats: they are called dogs because, when alarmed, they bark like terriers. They live in huge colonies called towns, often numbering thousands of burrows. Females produce litters of three or four young, in nests within the tunnels. When several give birth around the same time, the young are brought up together like a big family.

Musk Ox

Musk oxen, so called because of their musty smell, form family herds of a dozen or so adults on the Arctic tundra. The calves, born into the bitter cold of an Arctic spring, browse alongside their parents and shelter between them from the wind. There is a hungry wolf prowling around this herd, so the adults have formed a ring facing outward, with the calves in the middle. Musk ox horns are a match for any wolf.

• Family Life •

Safety in numbers

Young people feel safer and happier with friends or family around. In much the same way, other mammals and birds feel safer when there are others of their kind nearby. These may be immediate family (parents, brothers, sisters) or more distant relations. The important thing is that together they form a group with similar objectives – feeding, sleeping, attack, defense, and migration. Different kinds of animals make up different kinds of groups in which their young can live and learn safely. Prairie dogs (opposite page) live in huge extended family colonies on the grasslands of North America. They are actually rodents, but they bark like dogs when danger threatens. This mother has

spotted a prairie hawk and is barking a general warning that other mothers echo, sending all the rest scurrying to safety below. Similarly, capybaras warn one another of danger with shrill barks so they can dive for cover. Musk oxen make themselves into a threatening barrier between the young and the intruder. Dolphins keep their young safe by staying between them and the predator. African elephants surround the young when danger threatens, too.

A mother prairie dog (left) barks a warning to others in the colony as she catches sight of a predatory hawk in the air.

When danger threatens, the young cluster together and the adults form a protective barrier around them.

Capybara

Adult capybaras look like enormous guinea pigs. They live in groups along rivers and streams in South American rainforests. Capybaras produce litters of four to eight young. When several females give birth at about the same time, the piglets run together in a commune. All the mothers seem to care equally for them. When alarmed by predators, the mothers give shrill warning barks. Then they and all the piglets dive to safety under the water.

Bottlenose Dolphin

Here are a group of bottlenose dolphins protecting their young. Like most other dolphins, bottlenoses hunt in groups of a dozen or more, sometimes congregating into huge mobs of several hundred. The more adults there are, the better the slower-moving young dolphins are protected.

African Elephant

Herds of elephants wander across the dry plains of east Africa, in a constant search for fresh vegetation and water. Among the 9-foot-tall (3 m) adult elephants trot recently born young, each clinging with its trunk to its mother's tail, and only just big enough to keep up with the herd. When danger threatens, the little ones gather in the middle of the herd. The adults face outward with trunks and ears waving, ready to fend off hungry lions or hyenas.

Mother elephants giving birth to their single babies are often accompanied by a second female, who stands by to protect the mother and infant during and immediately after the birth.

Family Life

Living in groups

Living in extended family groups offers many advantages for young mammals and birds, including better protection, better chances of regular food, and more chances to learn both from the grown-ups and from each other. To survive in the groups, the young animals have to follow certain rules and codes of conduct. No-one teaches them, but they learn by trial and error as they go along. It pays young animals to be submissive to the older ones and keep out of quarrels.

The four timber, or gray, wolf cubs in northern Canada (opposite page) are leaving the family den for the first time. Just one month old, now they have to learn the pack rules. They will learn to run and hunt, to let the leader eat first, and to wag their tails cheerfully when approaching friends, but keep them low when the boss is around. Young hyenas, hunting dogs, and lions that live in groups all have to learn the same kinds of lessons.

Single wolves can manage on their own when there is plenty of food around, but family groups working together have a much wider range of foods. These wolves could not attack this old caribou singly. Together, they can surround and confuse it, keeping a safe distance from those sharp antlers. When the caribou tires, they will move in and kill it. The whole wolf pack will then enjoy a meal.

Spotted Hyenas

These young spotted hyenas are part of a pack hunting on the African plains. They are neither strong enough nor fast enough to hunt alone. But a pack running together can bring down all the food they need.

African Lions

A family group of lions, called a "pride," usually includes one large, dominant male, and two or three lionesses with their cubs. The lionesses do most of the hunting, working in small groups to chase and kill their prey. The leader and any other males protect the group from outsiders.

The lion leader, with his impressive mane and commanding roar, protects his family group.

Hunting Dogs

Rough-haired, with big round ears, they look like mangy domestic dogs. In fact, they are young hunting dogs – wild dogs that live in packs of a dozen or more on the east African plains. With long legs for running and sharp teeth for biting, they hunt by stalking groups of grazing animals, creeping through the long grass in search of young or injured animals. These three have found a young zebra and chased it several miles. Now they are closing in for the kill. They and their family will feed well on zebra meat before sundown.

Timber Wolves

The little wolf cub here has a lot to learn. It will soon be going out with its brothers and sisters to run with the pack. They will find that tail-up means a cheerful "hi" to their friends, but a threat to elders, especially the leader. In this way they learn to live and work together with as little trouble as possible.

Dolphin

Among the most lively and intelligent animals, dolphins are intensely sociable, living together and taking a great deal of interest in each other. We call groups of dolphins "schools." This is appropriate because they seem to be always squeaking and chattering among themselves, and reacting to each other like playful children. Some kinds of squeaks are for hunting, others for just keeping in touch with each other as the school moves through the sea.

Family Life
Wild school

The word "school" suggests a safe, sheltered place with teachers who teach and pupils who learn. Young animals, particularly those that live in groups and need to learn hunting skills, gain a kind of schooling during the first months of their lives. There is no formal teaching, but a great deal of learning from experience. The newborn bottlenose dolphin (opposite page) is learning an important lesson – how to breathe. Just a few seconds after birth, the adults are nosing it up to the surface, where it will open its blowhole for the first time and take a deep breath of air. Later it will learn from adults how to find fish, how to catch them, and how to hide among the bigger dolphins when sharks are around.

Similarly, the young koala, panda, and spider monkey (left) learn to feed themselves by sampling what their parents are eating. Young anteaters learn the tricks of catching ants, and young leopards learn survival both from their parents and from playfighting with other youngsters.

Koala

Koalas live in the forests of Australia, feeding on the leaves and shoots of eucalyptus trees. For most of the time, individuals stay apart from each other, so a baby koala learns mainly from its mother. At five to six weeks, a cub can be left to sleep safely by itself in the fork of a tree.

The young spider monkey quickly learns how to hang from a branch by the tail, using its hands to pick fruit.

Young pandas climb trees to escape danger. Later they grow too heavy, and have to hide in the undergrowth.

Giant Panda

Giant pandas live in the bamboo forests of southern China. Distantly related to bears, they munch all day on young bamboo shoots and grasses. Mothers produce single babies, which cling with all four limbs, first to the mother's stomach, then to her back. From there they lean over her shoulder to sample the foods she is eating – a safe way of learning.

Leopard

About five weeks old, this leopard cub is big enough to walk and explore its surroundings. There is much to learn. The lesson this morning is tree climbing. The cub is well equipped with strong muscles and claws, and a thick tail to help it balance. Before long it will be able to make leaps of 9 or 10 feet (3 m) and scramble around among the branches.

Giant Anteater

There is more to ant eating than you might think, and by watching its mother, this youngster is learning the tricks. First that long nose sniffs out an active nest. Then the big, powerful claws dig it open. Then the sticky saliva-coated tongue sweeps around the nest, pulling eggs, ants, and larvae into the narrow mouth.

A young anteater watches as its mother flexes her claws, ready to open an ant nest. Soon it will join in, and later go hunting for itself.

CHAPTER 2

Sharing

Most animals make their own way through the world. Some, like lions and antelope, can count on help from their own kind. Lions group together to hunt, while antelope group together to defend themselves against lions, finding safety in numbers. Gulls fly in flocks that increase their chances of finding food. Just a few species form partnerships with other kinds of animals – as you will see in this chapter.

There are many different kinds of partnerships, but they are never just the result of casual meetings. Some animals, like buffalo and zebra, can live quite successfully without each other, but come together because they share the same dangers, and benefit from each other's presence. Others, such as oxpeckers and shepherd fish, are seldom found alone. They are more successful when they live with their partners – oxpeckers with cattle, and shepherd fish with the jellyfish called Portuguese man-of-war. In some partnerships it seems quite clear that both partners benefit. Honeyguides, for example, lead honey badgers to wild bees' nests that the badgers might not otherwise find, and feed when the badgers have opened the nests. But not all partnerships seem as simple and clear-cut as that. Read about them, and see if you can spot how, in each of the examples, each partner benefits from the deal. Or do they?

On the Galapagos Islands in the Pacific Ocean, red crabs climb up from the sea to clamber over the backs of large lizards called marine iguanas. They feed on ticks and parasites that the iguanas cannot always get at themselves.

Clown Fish and Sea Anemone

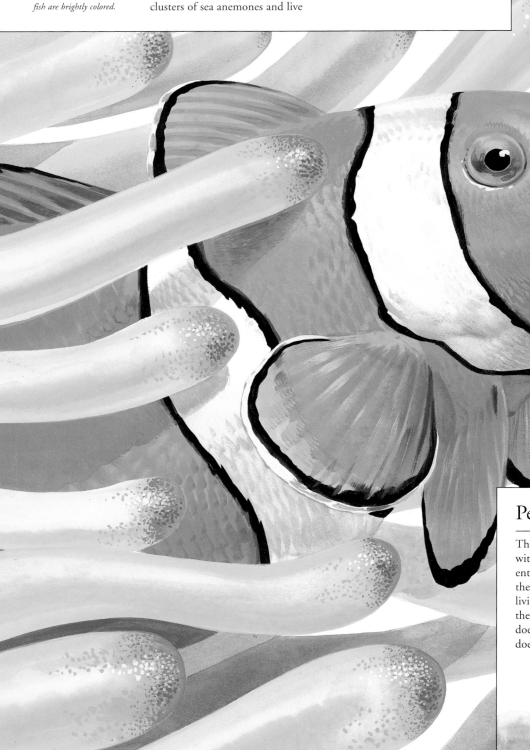

Like circus clowns, clown fish are brightly colored.

Clown fish, 3–4 inches (7.5–10 cm) long, live on coral reefs in warm tropical seas. Coral reefs are busy underwater "cities" where hundreds of species compete for food and space. Clown fish seek clusters of sea anemones and live among them, seemingly unaffected by the stinging cells of their tentacles, which paralyze and kill other fish. Each clown fish selects one particular anemone, from which it gains complete protection.

Pea-Crab and Mussel

This tiny crab, the size of a pea, finds safety within the shell of a blue mussel. It originally entered the shell as a larva, and then changed into an adult crab, living on fragments of food that the mussel collects on its gills. It doesn't eat much, and the mussel doesn't seem to mind.

Shield me

Life in the wild is full of dangers. Most animals throughout their lives are constantly at risk from hungry predators, parasites, and others that seek to kill or exploit them. For this reason they keep space around themselves, not allowing other animals of any kind to come near them. However, some species seem to have discovered that animals of another species can sometimes be of use to them, in quite unexpected ways.

This little orange and white clown fish (opposite page) lives among sea anemones, which lie with stinging tentacles spread waiting to catch and draw in passing food. Surprisingly, clown fish make their homes among the tentacles, darting in and out without being stung. Inside the ring of tentacles, they are safe from other predatory fish. Similarly, the shepherd fish lives among the tentacles of a deadly jellyfish, and fish called remora take rides on dangerous sharks. Pea-crabs and fish called bitterling each enjoy a different kind of association with mussels.

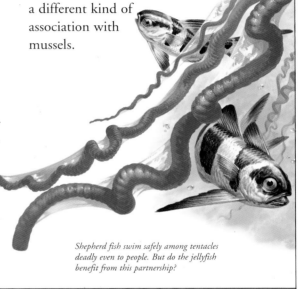

Bitterling

Bitterlings are freshwater fish, found in Europe and Asia, that lay their eggs in swan mussels. The female bitterling attracts a mate to a living, half-open mussel, and sheds a few eggs through a tube into the mussel shell. The male fertilizes the eggs, which then develop, protected by the mussel until they hatch and swim away. The mussel also gains from the deal. While the female bitterling is laying her eggs, the mussel sheds tiny larvae that bury themselves in the bitterling's surface. So, they get a free ride.

The clown fish finds a safe haven among the normally deadly tentacles of the sea anemone.

Shepherd Fish and Jellyfish

"Portuguese men-of-war" are jellyfish with gas-filled bladders that keep them afloat. Beneath each bladder hang bunches of tentacles up to 30 feet (9 m) long. As the jellyfish moves through the water, small animals are stung to death by the tentacles. Yet among the tentacles live shepherd fish that are quite unaffected by the stings. We don't know how they manage it, but they have found a safe haven from predators.

Shepherd fish swim safely among tentacles deadly even to people. But do the jellyfish benefit from this partnership?

Ramoras let go of the sharks to feed on other fish and then latch onto another host for free transportation.

Shark and Remora

Among the predators of the great oceans, there are none more likely to be hungry than great white sharks. Swimming in front of a shark would seem to be asking for trouble. But swimming just beneath one provides protection from other predators. These striped remoras, almost 3 feet (90 cm) long, do just that, attaching themselves to the underside of the shark or other large marine animal by the suckers on their heads. In return, they rid their host of parasites.

Working for meals

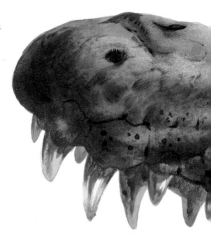

Most animals that feed on other species do just that – they hunt, kill, and eat other animals. Just a few species form life-long feeding partnerships with other kinds of animals, to the advantage of both. This Nile crocodile (right) grabs and kills small fish, birds, and antelopes that come within range, and could easily make mincemeat of the Egyptian courser sitting on its lower jaw. However, it chooses not to. The bird is pecking scraps of meat from between its teeth, a service that the crocodile probably finds comforting and refreshing – as you find when you brush your teeth.

Similarly, oxpeckers nibble at loose skin and parasites on a rhinoceros's back, and cod depend on much smaller wrasse to keep them clean. African honey guides call when they find a wild bees' nest, attracting honey badgers to the scene. The badgers follow the birds, find the nest, and open it with their strong paws. While they eat the honey, the guides eat their share of bees and larvae. Cattle egrets catch flies that fly up when cape buffalo stomp nearby.

Egret and Buffalo

Long-legged birds related to herons, cattle egrets live mainly in dry grasslands, feeding on flies and other insects that live among the grasses. The egrets stalk through the grass, stirring up insects and snapping at them as they go. Why cattle egrets? Because throughout North and South America, Australia, and other dry areas they have learned to move with herds of cattle, which stir up the insects for them. These egrets have found a herd of cape buffaloes, and are snatching at insects among their hooves.

Coral Cod and Wrasse

Several kinds of fish feed by cleaning scraps of skin and parasites from the surface of other fish. We call them "barber-fish" because they remind us of human barbers. Wrasse are a large family of fish – there are about 600 species altogether – with razor-sharp teeth, that feed mainly by nibbling and browsing over coral reefs and rocks. Some of the smaller wrasses have taken to barbering other fish, including both the skin and the inner surfaces of the mouth and gills. This tiny wrasse is foraging between the teeth of a brightly colored coral cod many times its own size. The cod doesn't seem to mind, and may benefit by being cleansed of skin parasites.

Honey Guide and Ratel

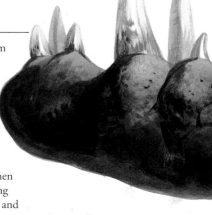

Honey is a nourishing food that bees make from nectar and use to feed both themselves and their maggot-like larvae. They store the honey in their nests. In the forests of Africa and Asia live small mammals called ratels, or honey badgers. Ratels feed mainly on berries, insects, and small reptiles, but are also fond of honey. In the trees nearby live small birds, called honey guides, that particularly like to eat bees and their larvae. When a honey guide finds a bees' nest, it gives a rattling call. The badger hears the call, follows the bird, and claws the nest open – so both can feed.

Rhino and Oxpecker

Oxpeckers are small birds of the starling family that live in small flocks on the African plains. When Europeans began farming in Africa, they saw these birds perching on their oxen, and called them oxpeckers. In fact, oxpeckers cling to many kinds of mammals, including giraffes, antelopes, and rhinoceroses like this one. They peck at ticks and other skin parasites, and snap up the biting flies that plague the mammals.

Crocodile and Courser

Coursers live mainly on insects, which they catch on tree trunks and in the air. However, this one has learned – perhaps in earlier life, by following a parent – that crocodiles have fragments of meat between their teeth, and do not snap at birds that sit close and clean them. The crocodile in turn has learned that it is not a bad thing to have a courser cleaning its teeth. The pecking may bring comfort or relief to its mouth. So coursers often clean crocodiles' teeth, and both benefit from the arrangement.

Coursers are plover-like birds that live in tropical Africa, Asia, and Australia. Nesting on the ground, usually near rivers or lakes, they feed mainly on insects. A crocodile lying at the edge of a lake or pond attracts flies and other insects, so a courser may find good hunting close to it, even on its back. A resting crocodile has no immediate interest in feeding, and may lie with its mouth slightly open anyway – so the courser is much safer than it looks.

Green Monkey and Gray Hornbill

Gray hornbills live in the dry savanna forests of South Africa, feeding on fruit and insects that they find among the leaves and branches. They share the treetops with bands of monkeys, including the green monkeys shown here. When a group of monkeys comes rattling through the trees, they dislodge insects and other small animals that gray hornbills like to eat. So the hornbills look out for the monkeys and follow them through the forest.

Zebra and Buffalo

Zebras live on the plains of east Africa in herds of a dozen or more. Buffalo too wander in small bands. Both may be attacked by lions, hyenas, or hunting dogs. Often they graze together in mixed groups. Like cows and horses, they feed slightly differently, so they do not compete. If predators attack, they defend themselves together.

Happy together

"Green" monkeys are usually yellowish-brown, with brown faces and white throats. They live in bands of a dozen or more, which gather in the treetops at night and spread out to forage during the day.

When animals of two different kinds come close to each other, there is usually trouble between them. One may be a predator, the other a possible meal. One may dominate the other, or move away in fear because the other comes too close. Yet two animals of different species can benefit strongly from keeping company.

Green monkeys and gray hornbills live together in the treetops of African forests. The monkeys feed on fruit, the birds on insects. Hornbills often follow the bands of monkeys, alert to the fact that as the monkeys scramble through the trees they disturb insects and make them easier to catch. Do the monkeys

benefit, too? Quite probably – they learn to respond to the hornbills' loud alarm calls, which may make the forest safer for them.

Two kinds of mammals, zebras and buffaloes, benefit from living together on the African plains, and so do two kinds of birds, bee-eaters and bustards. There are many such relationships among invertebrate animals, too. Here, a flying beetle and a false scorpion get together for mutual benefit.

Insects, disturbed by the monkeys, fly out – easy pickings for a hornbill.

The tiny false scorpions travel on the back of the flying beetle.

Scorpion and Beetle

False scorpions are closely related to true scorpions, but are much smaller and do not have a stinging tail. Like longhorn beetles (so called for their long antennae), they live in central South America. Longhorn beetles fly, but false scorpions can only walk on their short, stumpy legs. So the false scorpions hitch rides. This longhorn beetle carries several on its abdomen and in its wing cases. The false scorpions cause no trouble, and may even clean the beetle of parasites.

Bustard and Bee-Eater

Kori bustards are heavy turkey-like birds with wings spanning 7 feet (2 m). They live on the dry plains of east Africa, where they scratch the ground for insects and seeds. Carmine bee-eaters, much smaller birds, also live on the plains, catching bees and other flying insects. Often you will see bee-eaters riding on a bustard's back. The bustards raise swarms of flying insects, which the bee-eaters catch on the wing.

Bee-eaters make short flights from the bustard to catch flying insects.

Kookaburra and Termites

Rufous kookaburras are Australian kingfishers about 18 inches (45 cm) long. "Rufous" means reddish-brown, and "kookaburra" echoes their crazy, laughing call. Normally nesting in holes in river banks and hollow trees, they occasionally find a cavity in a termite's nest, which they enlarge to make their home. The termites probably don't know about it. They may even benefit, because the birds might deter unwelcome visitors.

Osprey and Night Heron

Among lakeside trees, you may see untidy tangles of sticks and seaweed – the nest platforms of ospreys, or sea eagles. With wings spanning 5 feet (1.5 m), ospreys live by catching fish on the water's surface. In spring, they often return to a former nest site, adding sticks and soft material. They would never allow birds of their own kind to share their nest, but sometimes tolerate other species. Here, a night heron, which fishes along the banks of streams, shares the platform under the osprey nest. Both will defend the nest against predators, so both gain protection from the arrangement.

Living Together
Tenants

Ant and Caterpillar

Large blue butterflies lay their eggs on wild thyme. When the eggs hatch, the caterpillars feed on the flowers, then fall to the ground and produce a sweet syrup, which attracts certain ants. The ants carry the caterpillars to their nest and

feed on the syrup. The caterpillars in turn feed on the ants' eggs, eventually leaving the nest as butterflies.

Making a home to bring up young safely can be hard work. Animal homes range from elaborate nests to simple dens, so long as they provide protection. Sometimes it pays an animal to take over someone else's home, rather than make one for itself. Sharing is another option, working well for both the host and the tenant. This rufous kookaburra (main picture) – a kingfisher-like bird of the Australian outback – has found a termite mound and hollowed out a part of it, moving in to lay her eggs.

Similarly, ospreys allow herons to nest

An ant carries off a young caterpillar of the large blue butterfly to tend in its nest.

on their large platform. They are not a threat, and may help to protect both nests from other invaders. Hermit crabs do not produce their own shells. Instead, they find an empty mollusk shell of suitable size and take up residence. Less amicably, a New Zealand shearwater may return home to find an unwelcome visitor in its burrow – a tuatara of uncertain temper that may even eat its young. One particular species of ant goes out to find a particularly desirable tenant, the caterpillar of the large blue butterfly.

Shearwater and Tuatara

Sooty shearwaters nest on islands off the coast of New Zealand, where tuataras – very rare lizard-like reptiles – also breed. The shearwater lays a single egg, usually in a burrow in soft, peaty soil. Tuataras often move into these burrows to lay their own eggs and raise their young – whether the shearwaters like it or not.

This male kookaburra brings back a small snake for his mate (top left).

Hermit Crab and Sea Anemones

Hermit crabs make no shells of their own, but live in the discarded spiral shells of whelks and other mollusks. Each young hermit crab finds a shell and squeezes in, graduating to bigger shells as it grows. Sea anemones often settle on the shells, helping to disguise them. The anemones may benefit from being moved around.

Kookaburras can kill snakes longer than themselves, grasping them and battering them to death on the ground.

CHAPTER 3

Fighting to Live

These are three kinds of tamarins – monkeys from the rainforests of southern Brazil, South America. About 12 inches (30 cm) long, with fat, bushy tails, they live high in the treetops, where their coloring blends with the strong light and shade of the forest. Tamarins live in small bands, each with their own kind – you would never see all three species on one branch like this. In fact you would be lucky to see any one of them in the wild, for all three are dying out, and dangerously close to extinction.

Like other small animals, tamarins have many predators that hunt and eat them, including jaguars and other cats, snakes, eagles, and owls. Despite this natural predation, they have continued to survive in the forests for hundreds of thousands of years. Within the last few hundreds of years, their most serious predator has been humans. Forest natives hunted tamarins for food. Then other humans came into the forests to trap and catch thousands of them to sell as pets. Most recently, a more serious danger threatens all three species. Their forests are being cut for timber and to clear the land for farming and building. That leaves the tamarins with only small patches of forest – they no longer have space to spread out, and will soon have nowhere to go.

Very few animals have easy lives. Practically all are constantly at risk from dangers within their surroundings, including predators, bad weather, and competition for space, nesting sites, food, and water. In the fight to live, strong claws and teeth sometimes help, but not always.

The monkey with the brilliant orange mane is a golden lion tamarin. On the left is a cottontop tamarin, on the right a moustached tamarin. All are seriously threatened in the wild. Very few of them remain in their native forests.

The fierce clash of horns between two bighorn rivals rarely results in serious injury.

Stag Beetles

Here is a wrestling match between two male stag beetles, each about 2 inches (5 cm) long. Called stag beetles because their jaws look like deer antlers, they rear up and circle round each other, each trying to grasp the other with its jaws. Eventually one succeeds, lifting the other into the air, and dropping it helpless on its back. Then the fight is over.

Bighorn Sheep

Bighorns are wild sheep that live high in the western mountains of North America. The ewes have small, spiky horns. Rams have much bigger horns, which curve downwards on either side of the head. These two rams have a problem to settle. The bigger one claims the hillside for himself and his ewes, while the smaller one also claims it. They argue by thumping their heads together. Those bony horns make a terrible noise, but there is no real damage. The smaller one will soon give up and find another patch of ground.

Fighting for space

African Lions

When the leader of a pride of lions is challenged by a younger male, the fight can be serious. They have sharp claws and teeth, and the loser may be badly damaged. When an old leader is defeated, he will slink away, perhaps to die. To the winner goes the leadership of the pride and the territory.

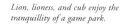

Lion, lioness, and cub enjoy the tranquillity of a game park.

Most animals need space around them, especially when raising a family. They claim their space, called a "territory," by moving in and defending it against others of their species. Some defend just the immediate area around their nest or den, to which they attract a mate. Some defend a bigger area in which they feed and rear their young. When animals of the same species fight, it is usually over territory. Many of the fights are a show of strength without bloodshed. The stronger wins, while the weaker withdraws.

European Robins

These "robin redbreasts" are birds of Europe and Asia. Both sexes have the prominent orange-red breast. In autumn, male and female robins take up separate territories, defending them with threat postures – pointing the bill upward to display the breast. In these territories they feed throughout winter. In spring, males and females are no longer rivals. Pairs get together, often from neighboring territories, to defend the much larger summer territories in which they feed and raise their broods.

These bighorn sheep (opposite) are quarrelling over territory. Each wants the hillside for himself and his family. The male kangaroos, too, are boxing to see who is the stronger. European robins display their colorful breasts as a first show of strength against an intruder, then attack if that fails. Male lions fight for control both of the land and of the lionesses in their group. Stag beetles wrestle solemnly when they meet, then go their separate ways. What are they fighting for? Only the stag beetles know.

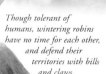

Though tolerant of humans, wintering robins have no time for each other, and defend their territories with bills and claws.

Red Kangaroos

These male red kangaroos of Australia, over 6 feet (2 m) tall, have found something to quarrel over, and are "kick-boxing" to settle the score. Grazing mobs, which include a dozen or more of both sexes, young and old, usually live peacefully together. Mature males fight most often over territory or females. Fights are seldom fierce, and the dense reddish-brown fur offers good protection, but many males bear scars from those powerful hind feet and sharp toenails.

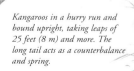

Kangaroos in a hurry run and bound upright, taking leaps of 25 feet (8 m) and more. The long tail acts as a counterbalance and spring.

Siamese Fighting Fish

These freshwater fish, only 2 inches (5 cm) long, are at home in south-east Asia. Early in the breeding season, the normally drab males (pictured right) become more colorful. Spacing themselves apart, each blows a small canopy of bubbles to make an upside-down nest on the surface. Each male, keeping others away with threats and attacks, invites females in to lay their eggs, which he then fertilizes and tends. The fish shown here are specially bred for combat.

In open ponds and streams, these fish threaten each other but seldom fight. Captive fish in tanks, where space is cramped, often damage or even kill each other.

Zebra

These zebras live on the plains of central and east Africa. Stallions (males) live most of the year in herds of young bachelors or in family herds led by a single older stallion. Young stallions sometimes invade the family herds. Here an old stallion uses his hooves to drive a younger one away. If the youngster wins, the herd will accept him as their new leader.

Battle for Life
Fighting for mates

Facing up to each other, jack hares box with their forearms, then leap over each other, striking hard with their hind legs. There is seldom a recognizable winner, but somehow these antics seem to determine which of the hares will mate most often with the watching females.

Male animals often need to be strong, and able to guard females and their young against ever-present dangers from predators. So males more than females tend to be fighters, sparring against each other to decide who is the strongest and likely to be the best and most effective mate. Fights over mates are most likely to occur early in the breeding season. They may look and sound fierce, but are not usually fights to the death. More often they are a show of strength in the presence of females. The winner stands his ground and keeps contact with the females. The loser disappears – until the next time.

These male Siamese fighting fish (opposite) spend much time threatening other males by swishing by and swirling jets of water at them. Brown hare bucks in spring put on a show of mad leaping, dancing, and kicking one another, with the does (females) looking on. The most impressive hare gets to mate with the most females. Male zebras, too, kick and bite each other, the dominant ones warning off the others. Jungle fowl attack competing males with their long, sharp leg spurs. Moose give a less energetic show of strength by pushing each other, head to head, intertwining antlers.

Brown Hare

Like large, long-legged rabbits, brown hares live widespread across Europe and Asia. They never burrow, but rely on their gray-brown fur to camouflage themselves. Male hares live quietly during the winter, but in early spring they gather in groups of up to a dozen, leaping and dancing as though demented, with the females looking on.

Jungle Fowl

These red jungle fowl live in the forests of southeast Asia. Males defend their females against the attentions of other males. In fighting, they leap into the air, striking downward with the bony spurs on the inside of their legs. After two or three "rounds," one retreats and the other crows to announce his victory.

Young hares, called leverets, lie quietly in the open, well camouflaged from passing predators.

Moose

Cow moose of northern Canada live throughout the year in small groups with their young. Bulls tend to be solitary, traveling around alone. Cows and bulls come together in September and October, when the bulls are wearing newly grown antlers and both are ready for breeding. Cows roar to attract the bulls, and the bulls fight in competition for the females. With lowered heads and antlers interlocked, rival bulls push backward and forward like overcharged steam engines. The one that pushes hardest and longest wins the females.

Largest of all the deer, bull moose stand over 7 feet (2 m) tall at the shoulder, and weigh more than 1,500 pounds (680 kg).

Chimpanzees

These two fighting chimpanzees belong to a band of 20 or 30 that roam through the west African forest in constant search for fruit, insects, and small animals to eat. Younger chimps that follow the older ones with respect have an easy time. This one has gotten out of line, maybe for taking too much food or wandering off on his own. The older, gray-faced chimp is teaching him a sharp chimpanzee lesson.

This young chimp has snatched an armful of fruit and is about to head off with it. If a hungry elder sees it, there will be trouble. The rule is: older animals eat first.

A young chimp may be punished, but there is little squabbling among members of a troop.

Battle for Life
Playfights and practice

King Cobra

King cobras are venomous snakes up to 7.5 feet (2.3 m) long. At the sight of prey, they rear up, ready to strike downward with poison-loaded fangs. Snakes are reptiles, with simpler brains than mammals and far less ability to learn. Hunting and striking at prey are inborn skills that quickly improve with practice.

Cobras start to hunt as soon as they are hatched. This one has caught a smaller snake.

At school or at home, children learn a lot about life through playfighting with friends or brothers and sisters. Playfights, which are usually quite harmless, teach us much about living together with other people, and how to look after ourselves. In the wild they are even more important. Many animals are born into very dangerous environments. From the start most have a built-in fighting ability, but they need to try out and practice their skills constantly before using them in earnest. A half-grown animal that cannot fight off enemies or bring down prey is unlikely to survive on its own.

The younger of the two chimpanzees (opposite page) is learning important lessons about who is boss and how to behave in a group. Timber wolves learn from each other how to fight and defend themselves, as do spotted hyenas. Elephants do not often fight – they are too big and it takes too much energy. But older ones know how to rough up younger ones that get out of line. King cobras are born killers, but improve their skills catching prey.

Spotted Hyenas

These young spotted hyenas are surveying a kill – an antelope hunted down by their pack on the African plains. They will have to wait for their share after the older hyenas have eaten, but it has been good practice for them. Spotted hyenas are the largest species of hyena, and as well as hunting in packs, a single hyena is quite capable of hunting down and killing an adult wildebeest.

Young spotted hyenas must wait their turn before they can eat.

African Elephants

African elephants live in groups that include several females with calves, and one or two young males. Older males wander alone, joining the herds when the females are ready to breed. Elephants keep in touch by throaty growling and purring and loud trumpeting. Young ones play together, rolling in the mud and mock-fighting – locking trunks and pushing against each other.

Timber Wolves

These two young wolves are playfighting. The one on top, with lips curled to show his formidable teeth, is winning. The other has surrendered, face turned away in submission. They are learning important lessons about living together from each other – how to show strength without damaging your opponent and how to submit to greater strength. Having learned these tricks of cooperation, each can play its part in the wolf team.

Learning to cooperate looks like a painful business, but the fighting is mostly for show, with no bloodshed or scars.

Claws

Claws are the horny, pointed tips that are grown by many land animals on the ends of their fingers and toes. We have nails, while cows and horses have hooves, but animals that climb or catch prey are better equipped with claws. How many? The basic number of fingers and toes is five per limb. Bears, for example, have five forward-pointing claws on each foot. But that is rather unusual. Most mammals that use claws for climbing or fighting have three or four on each foot, and nearly all birds have four – three pointing forward and one pointing backward.

Different animals use clawed fingers and toes in different ways. Claws are most useful for digging or grasping. The bear uses its claws for scraping soil and for slashing and grasping at prey. The barn owl's four great curved hooks will wrap tightly around a mouse, or dig deeply into a young rabbit. Lions, too, use their claws for grasping and holding, while koalas, like monkeys, use their claw-tipped fingers both for climbing and for the delicate handling of twigs and leaves. Jacanas, for their size, have the longest toes of any bird, tipped with claws, but use them for spreading their weight over water-lily leaves.

African Jacana

This strange-looking water bird breeds on the edges of tropical ponds and lakes. It feeds on

surface-living insects, which it catches by darting with its long bill. The lakes are often covered with water lilies and other vegetation on which the jacana walks. Those long, long toes with extended claws spread the bird's weight and keep it from sinking. When danger threatens, the male tucks the chicks under his wings and trots away. This one is hiding three chicks – you can see their clawed toes sticking out.

Jacana chicks, too, have long toes, extended by slightly curved claws, for walking on surface vegetation.

Koala

Koalas live in the dry eucalyptus forests of Australia. You seldom see one on the ground. The five-fingered hands and four-toed feet, fitted with strong, sharp claws, help them to climb upward, downward, and sideways along branches, looking for the fresh shoots and leaves that are their main food. Young koalas use their claws to hold tightly to their parents.

The koala's hand has five long fingers, the inner one almost thumb-like, all tipped with strong claws. It can curve delicately round a branch, or reach out to grasp shoots and leaves.

Like other cats, the lioness pulls her claws in when resting, but extends them to full length in a fight.

Lion

In a pride of lions, the dominant male leads the group, but the lionesses do most of the hunting. These two have stalked and caught up with a water buffalo – a huge and very strong animal that, in prime condition, would be a match for three or four of them. Perhaps it is old, injured, or tired. One way or another the two have cornered it. While one heads it off, the other has grabbed it by the shoulder and is holding on with teeth and claws. The claws, fully extended, dig firmly into the tough hide, and the lioness's weight pulls the buffalo to the ground. When the second lioness moves in, the fight will be over.

Bear

Bears of all species have five forward-pointing toes, making a broad, flat foot that takes their weight without sinking on soft ground or snow. The five strong claws, backed by the powerful shoulder and forearm muscles, are useful for digging through hard soil, snow, and ice, for tearing bark from trees, and for grasping and holding onto large prey. Fighting bears flatten their front paws, making formidable weapons edged with five sharp spikes. In fishing, they cup their paws, forming scoops that can flick a salmon from the water. Teeth and claws work together to skin and open dead animals.

Bears' claws grow continuously. Bears keep their claws sharp and trim by scratching on tree stumps.

Barn Owl

Pale, shy birds of forests and woodland edges, barn owls hunt in the half-light of evenings and early mornings. They hunt by sight and sound. Behind the mask-like feathers of the face are very acute ears, which allow them to find prey even in near-darkness. Like most other birds, they have dry, scaly feet. The four padded toes end in sharp, strongly curved claws – called talons – that draw together around their prey. A mouse, vole, or small bird caught in those talons would stand little chance of escaping.

Baboon

Baboons live in troops of up to 80 individuals, in which older males take the lead. They don't usually quarrel, so what is happening here? A young male (with his back to us) is trying to join the troop. The older one doesn't want him around. He has thumped the ground and shown a mouthful of threatening teeth. Now he is charging. There will be a scuffle and some angry squealing, and the youngster will run off. But he'll be back again tomorrow, as a full member of the troop.

• Claws and Teeth •
Teeth

Woolly Opossum

These small marsupial mammals of tropical forests from Mexico to Brazil live among the branches, feeding on leaves and insects. Woolly opossums live quietly, seldom meeting others of their kind or quarrelling among themselves. But they have 44 formidable teeth in their long jaws to defend themselves and their young against predators. (See also pages 28-29.)

Tiger

Tigers sleep through the heat of the day, hunting mainly in the evening and early morning. Like lions and other carnivorous animals, they have strong canine teeth – the four long ones at the front corners of the mouth – for grasping prey, with scissor-like cutting teeth on either side of the jaw.

Fingers and toes are tipped with claws, while jaws are lined with teeth. Humans have a total of 32 teeth – 16 in each jaw. Animals have anywhere from 2 to 60 or more. However many there are, teeth are used mainly for spiking, cutting, and grinding food.

This male baboon (opposite page) has cutting and spiking teeth in front, and grinding teeth at the back. But right now he is not thinking about food. He has curled back his lips and opened his mouth wide to threaten a rival with a show of teeth. The rival is showing his own teeth in reply.

Elephant tusks are two teeth of the upper jaw. They grow constantly throughout life, and are larger in males than females.

So teeth have another important use – in fighting and threatening to fight.

Woolly opossums have a long row of pin-sharp teeth that give a formidable bite. Tigers use their teeth mainly for tearing meat and crunching bones, but they also show them in threat displays. Elephants' tusks are huge, long teeth that grow throughout life, so they signify their owner's age and experience. Blue sharks have dozens of razor-edged teeth, set in rows around the edge of their mouths, and useful for just one thing – biting.

African Elephant

Elephants rarely fight. They use their tusks mainly to break down branches during feeding, and sometimes as weapons against predators. The tusks are also useful signals. Here two large males face each other – the nearer one, pawing the ground, can see at a glance that his rival is big, mature, and likely to stand his ground.

Shark

Of the dozens of different kinds of sharks, most are equipped with rows of small, very sharp teeth. Set edgeways in the skin of the mouth like triangular razor blades, they are constantly falling out and being replaced. An old shark's teeth are just as sharp as a young one's. In attacking prey, the shark uses its whole body. This blue shark has attacked a dolphin, stunning it and biting a piece from its side. Now it will turn and grasp the dolphin in its jaws, shaking, cutting, and breaking it into pieces.

With wide jaws and a mouthful of razor-sharp teeth, the blue shark has a lethal bite.

King Penguin

Second largest of all penguins, kings have large chicks that take more than a year to mature. As a result, they have to be kept on the colonies throughout winter. Thousands of chicks, each covered with dense brown down, huddle together to keep out the cold, while the parents forage in the bitterly cold sea for fish and squid. Hunting is difficult in winter. The parents have to swim many miles and dive deep, bringing food back to the chicks only at intervals of two to three weeks. Not surprisingly, many penguin chicks lose weight and die before spring.

Adult penguins have a covering of short, stiff feathers, with an underlay of down and a layer of fat under the skin. Females lay a single egg, which the parents take turns incubating for about eight weeks.

• Hard Living •
It's cold outside

Weddell Seal

Weddell seals give birth in September – early spring in Antarctica. Born on sea ice, this three-week-old pup is having its first swim. The mother has kept a hole open in the ice, so that she can dive into the sea to feed. When she dived in a few minutes ago, the pup followed. Now she watches anxiously as the pup figures how to get out.

For some animals "fighting to live" includes a fight against extreme cold. The world's coldest areas are the north and south polar regions and high mountaintops. Bitterly cold though they are, especially in winter, these regions are home to a surprising range of animals, from tiny insects to large mammals and birds. At temperatures below 32°F (0°C), rain turns to snow and water becomes ice. These areas are covered with ice and snow for much of the year. Polar regions are sunless for two or three months in winter, with correspondingly long spells of sunshine in summer. Polar animals have to fit their lives around these strange seasons. Mountaintops are usually colder than the plains below, and often intensely cold at night, even in the tropics.

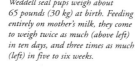

Weddell seal pups weigh about 65 pounds (30 kg) at birth. Feeding entirely on mother's milk, they come to weigh twice as much (above left) in ten days, and three times as much (left) in five to six weeks.

These king penguins (opposite page) live on the south polar island of South Georgia, where the chicks spend their winters in snowbound breeding colonies, and adults swim year-round in near-freezing seas. Weddell seals and wandering albatrosses are near neighbors, sharing the cold southern oceans. Polar bears and other kinds of seals inhabit the equally cold northern polar seas, and hardy mountain goats of several kinds live in the strange, cold habitats of the world's mountaintops.

Mountain Goat

Mountain goats are among the hardiest mammals, living high among the crags of mountains all over the world. Vegetation in these cold regions is sparse and often covered with ice or snow. To reach it they have to be sure-footed, browsing on the highest ledges and steepest, most slippery slopes.

Goats search a mountain ledge for a few shoots of grass.

Polar Bear

Polar bears live only on Arctic coasts, never far from the sea. Mothers produce their pups, usually twins or triplets, during the coldest months of winter, keeping them in a snow cave for the first 12 to 14 weeks. Emerging in early spring, the mother's first task is to find food – seals, fish, or other meat – to maintain herself and her furry cubs.

Polar bear cubs stay with their mother for up to two years, learning how to survive.

Wandering Albatross

Wandering albatrosses, with wingspans of 11 feet (3.4 m) or more, swoop over the southern oceans in a constant search for the fish, squid, and shrimp-like crustaceans that are their main foods. They nest on grass-covered islands in the cold southern Antarctic zone, rearing their single chicks through the gales, sleet, and snowstorms of winter.

This half-grown albatross chick has waited alone for several days for its meal of half-digested fish from its parent's throat.

• Hard Living •
Too hot for comfort

The hottest parts of the world are dry deserts. They are found in the tropical zone of every continent. Deserts are dry because they receive very little rainfall. They seem empty during the heat of the day. Yet they are still home to a surprising range of animals, including insects, reptiles, birds, and mammals. The fight here is to keep out of the sun as much as possible, and to secure water, which all animals need, both to drink and to keep themselves cool. Many of these animals sleep during the day – in caves, in burrows, under rocks, and anywhere

they can escape the hot sun. They feed mostly in the morning – when there may be dew on the vegetation – in the cool of the evening, and throughout the night.

Here are some animals from these dry desert regions. The pintailed sandgrouse (opposite page) lives in the deserts of central Asia, where there are no trees or shrubs to provide shade and the nearest water may be several miles away. The armadillo lives in deserts of southern South America, which are almost equally dry for most of the year. Prairie dogs

Armadillo

Armadillos are widespread in South America. The nine-banded species extends north into the southern United States. Though mammals, they have little fur. Instead they are encased in bony armor and tough, leathery skin. The nine bands on its back enable this species to curl into

Armadillos need little to drink, losing very little water through their dry, leathery skin.

a ball, a useful form of protection against coyotes and other predators. Living in hot deserts, armadillos spend their days in underground burrows and caves among the rocks, emerging in the evenings to hunt for insects, snakes, lizards, eggs, and similar food. This is also a time when moisture falls from the air as dew – often their main source of drinking water.

Prairie Dogs

Called dogs because they bark when alarmed, these little rodents live on the North American prairies. During the long, dry summers, the ground surface becomes uncomfortably hot. So the prairie dogs burrow underground (see pages 86–87), creating systems of tunnels in soil that remain cool even on the hottest day.

(not dogs at all, but rodents) inhabit the dry, grassy plains of North America, and gila monsters live in Mexico and the southeastern United States.

Living underground, for much of their time in the dark, prairie dogs recognize other family members by scent.

Gila Monster

This gila monster is just a large lizard, measuring 2 feet (60 cm) long fully grown, and covered with tough black and orange scales. It lives in desert lands of the southwestern United States. You may find one wandering abroad during the day. If so, don't touch it – it has a nasty bite. However, like other animals of hot deserts, it tends to hide away during the heat of the day. At night the air is both cooler and moister, and there are more animals around to provide supper.

The orange and black markings, worn even by newly hatched baby monsters, are a "do-not-touch" warning to other animals.

This male sandgrouse soaked his feathers in a pond several miles away, and brought back much-needed water to his thirsty chicks.

Pintailed Sandgrouse

These small birds of the grouse family inhabit sandy deserts. "Pintailed" refers to their sharply pointed tail feathers. They nest on open ground, laying three or four sandy-colored eggs that match their background well (below). The female birds take charge during the day, shading the eggs, and later the nestlings, from the searing heat of

the sun. Males take over for the evening and night shifts. Having spent the afternoon feeding on insects and seeds close to a pond, this one has brought water back in the feathers of his chest and belly, enough to cool the nestlings and quench their thirst.

Bird of Paradise

This male bird of paradise is dancing sideways along the branch, flicking his wings and orange plumes, bowing and swinging from side to side – showing off his finery to the much plainer yellow-capped female. If she is ready to mate, they will find a nesting site. The female will build a nest and lay three or four eggs, which she alone will tend, while the male sets out to attract other females. About 40 species of birds of paradise, the size of crows, live in the dense rainforests of New Guinea and Australia.

• Against the Odds •
Hunted to the edge

Manatee

They look and swim like unusually fat seals, but are grazers rather than hunters. Sailors call them "sea cows." Manatees live quietly in small family groups in warm, shallow waters of the Caribbean Sea, Gulf of Mexico, and neighboring rivers, feeding on sea grasses and water weeds. Young calves are at risk of being run down by speeding powerboats, and killed or injured by the propellers.

A newborn manatee (above), too heavy to float, is helped to the surface by its mother to take its first breath.

When explorers of Australasia in the 1500s first discovered species of these brilliantly feathered birds (opposite), and brought their skins back to Europe, everyone thought they could only have come from paradise – hence the name "birds of paradise." Native people who shared their forests already wore bird of paradise plumes in their robes and headdresses. Soon collectors and traders went there especially to trap the birds and take back their plumes for Europeans to wear. Hundreds of thousands of male birds of paradise were killed for their fine feathers. Some of the species have become very rare. As biologists say, they are on "the edge of extinction" – that is, in danger of disappearing altogether.

This book shows other animals that are close to extinction, such as the tamarins (pages 46–47). On these pages, you can read about the manatees, endangered because people drive powerboats through their breeding areas, disturbing, injuring, and killing the young. Bald eagles, the national emblem of the United States, are at risk because too many have been hunted, and more recently poisoned by chemicals in their breeding areas. Leatherback turtles are less plentiful than before, mostly through disturbance at their breeding grounds. With care, these animals can all be saved from extinction.

Leatherback Turtle

Adult leatherback turtles live in all the warm seas of the world. Up to about 6 feet (2 m) long, they feed mainly on jellyfish. Males spend their lives at sea. Females go ashore several times a year to dig nests in the sand and lay eggs. Seven weeks later, the baby turtles hatch, dig themselves out of the sand, and race down to the sea. Humans like to eat the eggs, and many other predators, such as this black vulture, wait to catch the baby turtles on their first journey.

A newly hatched leatherback turtle, 2 inches (5 cm) long, swims by the head of an adult.

Bald Eagle

A bald eagle feeds two hungry chicks. Once common over most of the United States, these eagles now survive mainly in wilderness areas of Alaska and Florida. Hunters and farmers killed many thousands in the early days of land settlement. More recently, chemical insecticides and poisoned baits have killed many more. Wherever they remain today, bald eagles are protected by law.

High on a tree trunk (left), a fully fledged chick leaves the nest for the first time, 12 weeks after hatching.

• Against the Odds •
Nowhere to go

Mountain Gorilla

How does a young gorilla learn which plants are good to eat, and which are too tough or poisonous? This one (opposite page) is learning fast. For the last few weeks she has been carried on her mother's back, where she can see the world ahead. She can watch other members of the troop, see insects, lizards, and birds, and keep an eye on the plants that her mother is eating. Though still feeding on her mother's milk, she will occasionally reach over and try some shoots, leaves, flowers, and fruit. Before long she will know what is good to eat.

Gorillas usually live peacefully within their own troops. With plenty of forest around them, they can live peacefully with neighbors, too.

Largest of all the apes, gorillas live in the hot, damp forests of central Africa. These two, a five-year-old mother and her five-month-old baby, belong to a troop of a dozen mountain gorillas. Led by a large elderly male, in company with other mothers and babies, they wander each day through the forest, looking for trees with the fresh shoots, leaves, and fruit that are their main diet. The forest has existed for tens of thousands of years, supporting many generations of contented gorillas. Now, times are changing for the animals, and life is becoming more difficult. Parts of the forest have been destroyed – cut down for

Orangutan

Orangutans live in the rainforests of Sumatra and Borneo. Like gorillas, they are apes, and both are closely related to man. Young orangutans are lithe and active, shinnying up the trees and swinging from branch to branch. Older ones grow heavy and less active, tending to remain near the ground. Old males also develop large cheek flanges (above). Like other apes, orangutans feed mainly on fruit, shoots, and leaves. Like others, too, they are at risk, because the forests are being cleared for timber, leaving less room for all the native animals.

timber and to clear the land for farming. What is left has become noisy with bulldozers, trucks, and chainsaws. There is less and less room for the gorillas that remain.

Much the same is true for other animals on these pages. Pygmy hippos, orangutans, and maned wolves are all in different ways coming under pressure from expanding human populations. People need their trees for timber, and their land or water for farming. People usually take what they want, leaving the animals with nowhere to go.

Young orangutans are sometimes captured and sold as pets. Small ones make friendly, responsive companions for children. As they grow older and stronger, they damage and break furniture and have to be caged (right). Sadly, that makes them mean and hard to handle.

Maned Wolf

These elegant, long-legged animals – closer to foxes than to wolves – live on the grasslands of southern Brazil and Argentina. We know little about them. They sleep during the day, emerging in the evenings to hunt for voles, mice, and other small mammals. Unfortunately for them, the grasslands are now farmed, and maned wolves also take lambs, chickens, and other domestic stock. So the farmers and ranchers hunt and shoot them on sight, and poison them in their dens. There are very few maned wolves left in the wild.

Like long-legged foxes, maned wolves roam the grasslands of eastern South America.

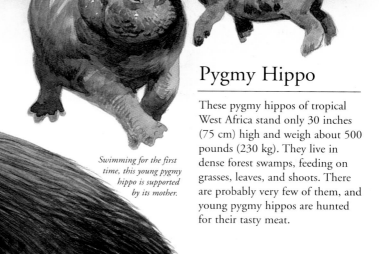

Swimming for the first time, this young pygmy hippo is supported by its mother.

Pygmy Hippo

These pygmy hippos of tropical West Africa stand only 30 inches (75 cm) high and weigh about 500 pounds (230 kg). They live in dense forest swamps, feeding on grasses, leaves, and shoots. There are probably very few of them, and young pygmy hippos are hunted for their tasty meat.

CHAPTER 4

Defenses

Life among animals is a balance of predators and prey. Predators – animals that hunt and eat other animals – make the attacks and call the shots. Prey – the animals that are hunted and eaten – are the intended or actual victims. We ourselves are predators, descended from long lines of hunters. As such, we relate more to animal predators than to prey. Predators we see as winners, prey as losers.

Yet prey, too, are winners. In the hard world of eat-and-be-eaten, any animal that survives to maturity has already won several "rounds." Any that survive long enough to leave offspring have won the game, for leaving offspring is what life is about. Prey win by tricks and strategies that we sum up as "defense." Defenders hold out in dozens of different ways, some obvious, others bizarre, and all remarkable for being inborn or innate.

This lantern fly from South America, for example, looks much like a dead leaf. Settling among dead leaves, it becomes almost invisible, camouflaged against its background. That is its first line of defense. If a predator approaches closely, the fly parts its wings to expose the two yellow-and-black spots that look like eyes. Scared, the predator decides to leave the lantern fly alone. Flashing its eyespots is the lantern fly's second line of defense. It is achieved quite automatically and with very little effort (see page 76).

This chapter is about defenses, defenders, and the many strange ways in which they increase the chances of survival for themselves and for their offspring.

Experimenters using different patterns of crosses, dots, and rings have shown that birds are most frightened by the sudden appearance of spots that resemble the eyes of a mammal or bird.

Poison Arrow Frogs

Found in the tropical forests of South and Central America, these tree frogs live in tiny pools on tree branches, feeding on insect larvae and carrying their eggs and tadpoles on their backs. They contain strong nerve poisons, which native hunters extract and paint onto arrows. A lizard, bird, or monkey pierced or even scratched by a frog-poisoned arrow dies within minutes.

Fire-Bellied Toad

Many kinds of toads have skin glands that give them a nasty taste. This fire-bellied toad has additional reminders. Disturbed by a heron, it sits up and falls backward, exposing a bright red underbelly, at the same time producing a smelly and foul-tasting fluid. However absentminded, the heron is unlikely to forget the message – fire-bellied toads are frightening, trouble, horrible to taste, and best left alone.

The yellow frog is poisonous to touch. From poison arrow frogs of other colors, native Indians extract poison to paint on their arrows.

Watch out: I'm poisonous

Animals defend themselves in many ways. Some show their teeth and snap, others run away, still others simply disappear. These little tree frogs (opposite), each about 2 inches (5 cm) long, defend themselves by wearing bright colors. It may not seem an effective kind of defense – wouldn't they be better off hiding? Not really, because they have two secret weapons – they carry poison and they taste very unpleasant. Any animal that tries to grab one gets at least a nasty flavor in its mouth, at worst a dose of poison that may kill it. A young bird or mammal might try it. Older ones that have tried – and lived to

remember the experience – will keep clear of frogs in carnival dress.

Fire-bellied toads give the same kind of warning. So do the caterpillars of monarch butterflies and tiger moths, and many other brightly colored animals. Think of yellow-and-black-banded wasps, hornets, bumblebees, and a dozen other familiar garden insects. Think of gila monsters (page 60), frilled lizards (page 70), and brightly colored snakes (page 76). One way or another, they are all warning predators: lay off, or catch a nasty surprise.

High among the leaves of a rainforest tree, two blue poison arrow frogs that seem to be wrestling are actually courting (right). Their vivid coloring, like that of the other frogs, is a warning to birds, snakes, and other predators not to touch them.

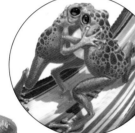

When danger threatens, the garden tiger moth exposes its orange-and-black underwings.

Garden Tiger Moth

Both the garden tiger moth and its caterpillar (see page 13) contain poisons. Any bird trying to eat either one would end up with indigestion or worse. The moths have bright orange hind wings, hidden at rest but flashed at the least sign of danger. This is a warning that predators are likely to note and remember: this thing is not good to eat.

Monarch Butterfly

Monarch butterflies are easily recognizable, with brilliant patterns on both sides of their wings. Their caterpillars, almost 2 inches (5 cm) long, are colorfully striped. Both butterflies and caterpillars are poisonous to predators. The caterpillars gather their poison from the sap of the milkweeds on which they feed. Though harmless to them, it causes vomiting or death in predators. The bright colors are a reminder and a warning.

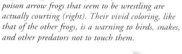

Back off: I can hurt

Bright coloring is one form of warning. A sudden change in shape is another. And presentation of weapons is a third. This porcupine fish (opposite) combines all three. There are several kinds of porcupine fish, all living in shallow seas and estuaries. Up to 2 feet (60 cm) long, they stay close to the seabed, feeding on clams and other shellfish, which they crunch with strong, bony jaws. When danger threatens, they suck in water and blow themselves up – into a brightly colored balloon covered with spikes, which a predator would

have great difficulty tackling.

Porcupines, after which these fish are named, are mammals with a similar trick to make themselves look bigger. Covered with hundreds of quills – stiff, pointed hairs – they respond to danger by making every hair stand on end, almost doubling their size. Frilled lizards spread a colored ruff around their necks. Hippopotamuses yawn, displaying an enormous mouth with peg teeth – enough to make any predator think twice about causing trouble.

Porcupine Fish

Porcupine fish are covered with scales, each ending in a sharp, bony spine. Normally they look much like other fish, unusual only in their spiny covering. When a

The porcupine fish (above) pumps itself up (right) at the sight of a predator.

predator – perhaps a bigger fish – comes into view, they take in water, pumping themselves up into near-spherical balloons, with spines sticking out in all directions. They tread water, turning to keep the predator in sight. When danger passes, they release pressure and return to normal.

Frilled Lizard

This lizard from northern Australia, 30 inches (75 cm) long, normally looks like any ordinary lizard. But when threatened, it spreads an untidy-looking neck scarf into a dazzling orange collar, then opens its mouth to reveal a vivid pink or blue lining. At the same time, it steps forward and hisses – a display startling enough to scare away any predator.

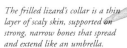

The frilled lizard's collar is a thin layer of scaly skin, supported on strong, narrow bones that spread and extend like an umbrella.

Porcupine

Here a cougar has met an African brush-tailed porcupine and is sizing it up as a possible breakfast. The porcupine has met cougars before and is wary. First it turns away and presents its backside. Then it raises its quills and rattles them, making itself look twice as big and producing an alarming noise. Finally, if still uneasy, it will run backward toward the cougar and perhaps spike it with some of its longer quills. The cougar will find this very uncomfortable and possibly worse, for the quills can dig in and become poisonous.

This cougar may end up with a faceful of quills, and a lesson it will never forget.

Hippopotamus

Hippos live in small groups in muddy rivers of tropical Africa. On hot, sunny days they lie submerged, with only eyes, ears, and nostrils above the surface. Should a rival hippo appear, the resident male opens his mouth wide. Is it just a yawn? No, it's a threat – those teeth could do all kinds of damage in a fight.

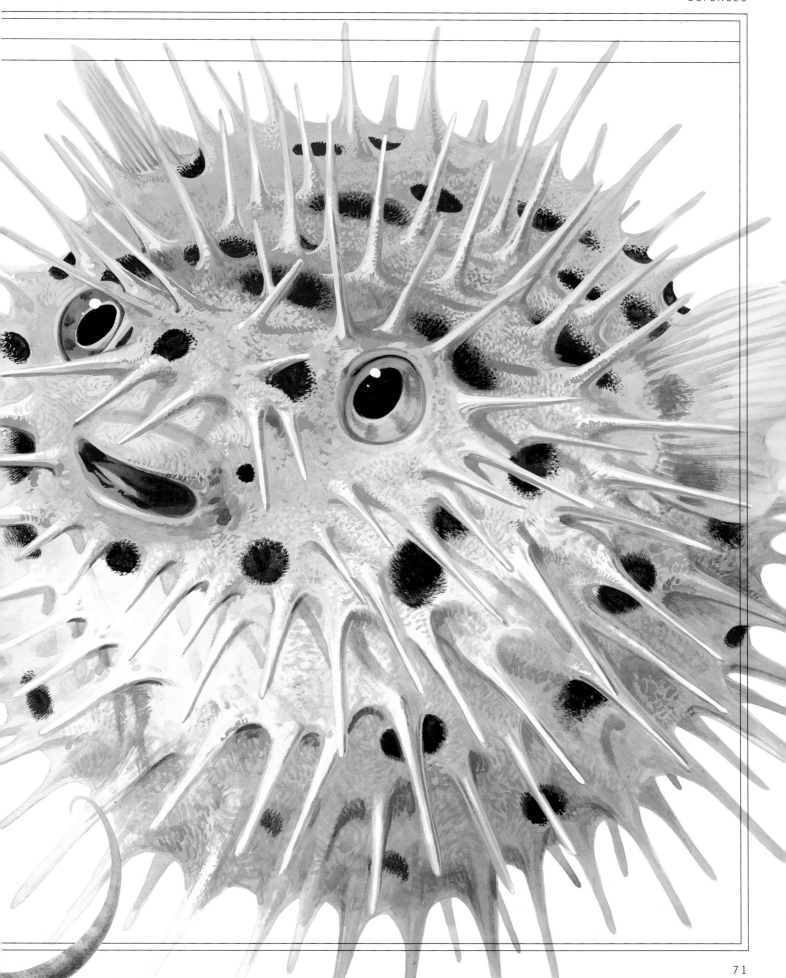

Armadillo

Armadillos are found in the dry grasslands of South and Central America and the southern United States (see page 60). This one has met a coyote, a fox-like predator that is ready to eat practically anything, including armadillos. This armadillo ran surprisingly fast on its short legs, but the coyote ran faster, cutting it off from its burrow. So the armadillo has stopped and curled up into a ball. The coyote knows that there is something inside there to eat – he was chasing it just a couple of minutes ago – and is figuring out how to get in. He will soon lose interest, and wander off to look for more cooperative prey.

The coyote cannot unravel this armadillo puzzle.

You'll get nowhere with me

Spotted Skunk

Widespread in the woodlands of North America, spotted skunks announce their presence by a strong, sharp smell. It is always with them, based in a liquid produced by two glands under the tail, which they can shoot out to a distance of 10 feet (3 m). Threatened by a cougar, this skunk has turned tail-on, raised its hind legs, and is about to shoot. The cougar will smell of skunk for days.

Sooty Albatross

This sooty albatross chick (below left) was left sitting alone on its nest on a cold sub-Antarctic island. Both parents are away searching for food. The skua, a predatory gull-like bird, has moved in to attack. The chick retaliates by vomiting up a jet of evil-smelling oily liquid – the remains of its last meal – from its throat.

Here are two more ways of dealing with predators. One is to tuck yourself in a bony, box-like wrapping that no predator can undo – like sitting in a strong room to which only you have the key. The other is to produce some horrible smelly substance that puts predators off forever.

Most reptiles have scaly skins, tough but flexible enough for the animal to move comfortably inside. Tortoises and turtles have settled for a skin lined with bony plates – still covered with scales, but box-like, hard, and unyielding – surrounding the whole body. Slots in the back and front allow them to draw in their limbs, tail, and head. It is a well-tested form of defense – there have been tortoises in the world for over 200 million years.

Most mammals have soft skins, fur-covered and flexible. Armadillos and pangolins have different forms of armor-plating, flexible so they can move around, but too tough for a predator to open. Both curl up when attacked, making themselves into impenetrable balls. Skunks and albatross chicks, by contrast, use chemical warfare to fend off attackers.

The pangolin's tough scales protect it from the bites and stings of ants, and also from the teeth and claws of foxes, cats, and other predators.

Desert Tortoise

This desert tortoise lives in a box formed from broad ribs, bony plates, and a tough, horny shell. When it senses danger, it pulls legs, head, and tail into the box. To the fox, which is both hungry and thirsty, it would make a welcome meal. Its meat contains more water than the fox could find for miles around in the desert. But the fox might as well give up and go looking for mice, lizards, or insects, instead.

If the fox comes closer, the tortoise will settle and pull itself into its shell.

Pangolin

It looks like a fir cone on legs, but is actually a pangolin, or scaly anteater, a mammal of tropical Africa and Asia. It is covered with scales instead of hair. Pangolins feed on ants, opening their nests with those powerful claws, sticking that long nose in, and licking up the ants with a sticky tongue. The scales protect them from ant bites and also from predators. When threatened, the pangolin rolls into a tight ball, and if disturbed, squirts the predator with jets of urine.

Virginia Opossum

"Playing possum" means pretending to be dead. "Possum" is short for "opossum." Virginia opossums are the animals that gave rise to the saying. If grabbed by a predator, such as this bobcat, the opossum scratches and bites, then suddenly goes limp as though dead. Why doesn't the bobcat eat it? Because for bobcats, like many other hunters, hunting and feeding are separate activities. When the hunt is over, they lose interest until they feel ready to eat. That is the opossum's chance to sneak away.

This American Virginia opossum is "playing possum" – it has stopped struggling and gone limp. The bobcat will soon lose interest, and the opossum will walk away.

Crocodile

Five seconds ago this African Nile crocodile was floating like a log on the lake, with only eyes, nostrils, and brown, scaly back above the surface. The springbok, coming down to drink, saw it but took no notice – it thought it was just another log. Now the "log" has

sprung into action, with jaws open and teeth ready to grab. The springbok has about half a second to leap into the air and skip away.

Great actors

Mimicry is imitation. Acting is the kind of imitation we see on the stage or on television, where people play at being other people – heroes and gangsters, good guys and bad guys. In a similar way, many kinds of animals imitate each other in appearance or behavior. Without knowing what they are doing, without learning a part or rehearsing, they can be surprisingly good actors. They use acting to grab a meal, get themselves out of difficulties, or even save their lives.

Some look and act like fiercer or more dangerous animals – there are several examples of these throughout this book. Some, like the Virginia opossum in the main picture here, simply play dead, so that predators will lose interest and leave them alone. Some stay very still, as though they were logs or part of the scenery – the crocodile and Komodo dragon are good examples. Some, like the woodcock and ringed plover, stay still for a time, then act as though they were hurt or damaged, attracting hunters toward them – and away from their nests.

Ringed Plover

Nesting on bare Arctic gravel, ringed plovers are liable to attack by foxes. If one approaches, the sitting bird stays absolutely still. If the fox comes closer, it leaps up and totters from the nest with wing trailing, shrilling alarm calls. The fox chases, and the plover leads it away from its eggs or nestlings.

Komodo Dragon

Komodo dragons – giant lizards up to 10 feet (3 m) long – live on the tropical islands of Indonesia. This one has been lying still at the edge of the forest, waiting for breakfast. The monkey, a young macaque, has swung down from the trees to investigate. As it came within reach, the lizard reared up with jaws open and claws grabbing. The monkey may just be lucky and get away.

Komodo dragons are meat-eaters with a taste for monkeys. If this macaque escapes, it will keep its distance in the future.

Woodcock

Woodcocks are handsome birds, richly barred in black, gold, and brown. On the nest they sit very still, mimicking their background so well that predators seldom see them. This is their first line of defense. Their second is to mimic an injured bird. Like the ringed plover (above left), they stagger up with wing trailing, calling as though in distress, attracting the predator's attention and leading it well away from the nest.

Looks that lie

Many insects are effective mimics, looking and acting like plants, other insects, or merely dull objects of no particular interest. Predators use mimicry to attract and capture their prey. Species that are themselves prey use mimicry to confuse their hunters, perhaps by mimicking the color, form, and actions of other animals that are feared or avoided by their predators.

The orchid mantis of the main picture is an insect that almost perfectly mimics the elegant, elaborate shape and clear color of a particular species of orchid. This enables it to sit in the flower that it mimics, to catch and eat unsuspecting insect visitors.

Geometrid moths are almost identical in size, shape, and color to the dying leaves of the particular shrubs they inhabit. Lantern flies are moths that look remarkably like dead leaves, but flash pretend eyes on their hind wings if predators come too close. Sawflies and milk snakes, both relatively harmless, mimic other animals with stronger and more positive defense mechanisms.

Orchid Mantis

Here is an insect of Indonesia and Malaysia that remarkably resembles a flower. Mantises are leggy insects with long, slender bodies, short wings, and elaborately folding limbs. They catch and eat other insects, and specialize in living on pink and violet orchids. To mimic the orchids, they have developed broad flanges of exactly the right shape and color on their limbs, and their wings, head, and abdomen are all tinted in matching shades of pink and violet.

True wasp

Sawfly

This yellow-and-black creature (below left) buzzes like a wasp (above left) and is colored like a wasp, and its rear end looks like a stinger. But it is not a wasp – it is a giant horntailed sawfly, and it does not sting. The long tail is an ovipositor, for dropping eggs into holes drilled in bark. Birds learn by experience to avoid wasps, so being a wasp look-alike gives the sawfly a measure of protection.

Giant horntailed sawfly

Which snake is to be avoided? Remember the rhyme: "Red against yellow, dangerous fellow."

Lantern Fly

This South American lantern fly (above) – so called because some of its relatives flash light from their noses – matches a wide range of vegetation backgrounds. Matching is its main defense against predators. But touch it lightly, and it will partly spread its wings, revealing two spots that look remarkably – even frighteningly – like the eyes of a predatory mammal or bird. Experimenters have shown that, of all symbols, birds are most frightened by the sudden appearance of eyes. So flashing eyespots is an effective way to scare them off.

Coral Snake, Milk Snake

Most snakes blend with their background. These snakes from the southern United States are conspicuous in red, black, and yellow stripes. The smaller one, an Arizona coral snake, has a bite that is deadly to birds and small mammals. As with other venomous reptiles, it pays for them to be seen and avoided. The larger Louisiana milk snake looks very much like the coral snake, but has no venom. It probably benefits by looking dangerous, even if it isn't.

Insects hovering nearby, attracted by the orchid's scent, are grabbed by the mantis's long forelimbs, overpowered, and eaten.

Geometrid Moth

There are thousands of kinds of moths, all with different needs for display and camouflage. Some need to be highly colored, to attract mates and blend with flowers. This geometrid moth specializes in looking as inconspicuous and ordinary as possible – like a dead leaf on a pile of dead and decaying leaves. Why? Possibly because it lays its eggs on leaf litter, and is safer from predators when it blends in. It would take a sharp-eyed predator to spot this one. Other moths of its kind look like tree bark, moss clumps, or bird droppings.

To hide, this moth just has to land among the right kinds of leaves, which it recognizes by sight or scent.

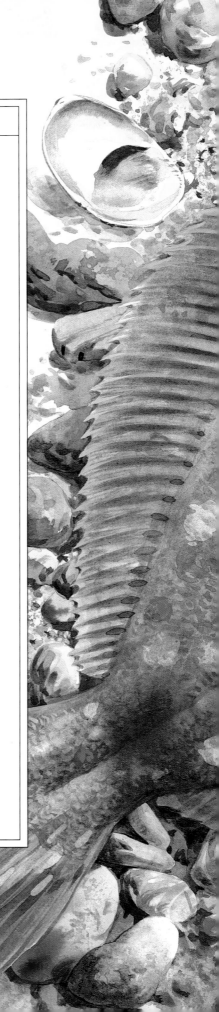

CHAPTER 5

Now You See Me ...

In the world of humans, every day thousands of adults warn young people to stop showing off, while thousands of others tell them to go out and make their mark. Animals are no less confused. Some show off madly as part of their daily lives, while others hide away and live as quiet and undisturbed a life as possible.

Among show-offs, it is usually the males that make the most fuss, singing from the treetops, wearing vivid colors, or dancing up and down. Biologists call it "display," but that is just another name for showing off.

In contrast, there are the animals that go to great lengths to live quietly and keep to themselves for most of the time. Some hide so that predators cannot find them, others so they can jump out at prey to become predators themselves. In species with show-off males, females remain drab and relatively silent. But with so many predators around, isn't it dangerous to be a show-off?

There are good reasons for showing off. Lions roar and wolves howl to hold their families together and warn others that they are near. Male frigatebirds wear red "balloons" to attract females, and poison arrow frogs wear bright colors to warn that they are dangerous. But there are good reasons, too, for lying low and matching your background, like this colorful but well-camouflaged plaice on the seabed.

This plaice, lying flat on the gravelly seabed, has the ability to change color to match its background as it moves around.

Magnificent Frigatebird

Frigatebirds nest on tropical oceanic islands from the eastern Pacific Ocean to the Caribbean Sea and west Africa. When a male is seeking a mate, he spreads his black wings, throws back his head, and inflates a balloon of red skin under his throat, a display that attracts females flying overhead. Here, a female has landed, and is considering the situation. It will not take long before the two birds mate, and a single large egg is laid.

Once courtship is over, the skin of the throat contracts and the balloon disappears – packed away until the next breeding season.

Imperial Angelfish

These brilliantly striped fish live among tropical coral reefs. Dozens of other kinds of fish, with different color patterns, share the reefs. These bars and patches are not camouflage colors. The different patterns are displays that help every fish to recognize its own kind unerringly. Young fish learn their own pattern in their first few hours after hatching, when the closest objects are fish of their own kind. They will be able to recognize their own species for the rest of their lives.

• Showing Off •
Look at me

Toucan

Some 35 different kinds of toucans share the rainforests of South and Central America. They need to look markedly different from each other. This sulfur-breasted toucan's colors attract only females of his own kind.

For different reasons, many animals need to draw attention to themselves. In effect, they are shouting, "I am important, look at me," though they don't always shout. They may roar or whistle. They may wear bright feathers or striped tails. Or they may emit clouds of perfume.

As these pages show, displays can take many forms.

Bright colors help this male sulfur-breasted toucan to get himself noticed by a female of his own kind. The ring-tailed lemurs live in family groups, settling disputes by flashing their bushy, elegantly striped, scent-carrying tails. In a group of mandrills, the leader's vivid red-and-blue facial coloring says, "I'm the boss." The colorful stripes of the imperial angelfish alert the young fish to their parents' presence. Male frigatebirds gain their mate's attention by blowing up their pouch, a large red balloon under the bill.

Toucans feed on insects and fruit. The huge bill, one-quarter the length of the bird, is well shaped to search the bushes for food, and its distinctive colors help to advertise the bird's species.

Mandrill

Female mandrills are dull brown. Only adult males are colorful. Why? Mandrills live in small family troops, several of which may live and forage together. Disputes that arise are settled by displays among the leaders. These are the biggest male mandrills,

Ring-Tailed Lemur

Ring-tailed lemurs live in the forests of Madagascar and neighboring islands, in troops of a dozen or more that include adult males and females, and offspring. Each troop keeps to its own part of the forest. If you see a gathering of lemurs, some standing with tails upright, others sitting and watching, it is probably a peaceable border dispute between two troops from neighboring territories. Before raising their tails, the lemurs whisk them across glands on their arms, impregnating them with distinctive musky scents. Each troop asserts its claim by wafting its own scents over the others.

distinguished by bright red-and-blue faces and blue backsides. When the biggest male faces the group, lesser mandrills get the message. When the big one walks away, with backside glowing like a light in the forest, the lesser ones follow.

Temminck's Tragopan

Males of this species are vividly colored, with horn-like tufts of feathers above their eyes and brilliant wings and bibs. To attract a female, a male must also be active. He runs around her in a circle with the near wing down – like a banking aircraft – then races toward her with feathers raised, and dazzles her with a display of shaking and quivering.

• Showing Off •
Winning dances

Birds are among the world's greatest show-offs. Feathers contain colored pigments, and some split light on their surface to create iridescent colors. Different shapes of feathers make tufts, patches, and patterns, and birds can pack extra color into their bills and legs. Their reasons for brilliance vary. In tropical forests, vivid colors are muted in the light and shade of the canopy. Bright colors often distinguish one gaudy species from other equally, but differently, gaudy birds. Many kinds use gaudiness in courtship, colorful males displaying to less colorful females.

Temminck's tragopan is brilliant standing still. Imagine it leaping in a courtship dance. Golden pheasants, too, dance wildly in courting, umbrella birds more sedately, with neck feathers raised like a parasol. Male lovely cotingas (yes, that is their name) display even after courtship, diverting attention from their mates, nest, and eggs. Male fiddler crabs are crustaceans, not birds, but they also dance with claws clicking and waving to win over mates.

Lovely Cotinga

Lovely cotinga males of Central America, in dashing purple-blue plumage, glow in the forest sunlight. The females' darker plumage merges with the vegetation. During courtship, the males show off in competition in

front of the females, flashing madly back and forth in a spectacular line dance. The females view them critically, then make their choice. After mating, the females alone take care of nests, eggs, and chicks, while the males continue to show off. In drawing attention to themselves, they keep predators away from the vulnerable nests.

Fiddler Crab

These orange crabs live on tropical seashores. Adult males have one vastly enlarged claw, which they hold under their chin like a violin, or fiddle. During courtship, when the tide is out, the males wave their fiddles rhythmically in the air, sometimes clicking simultaneously like a crazy orchestra. To other males, the waving means "Keep away." To females, it signals, "Come over and see me." The fiddles are used also in fighting, when the males hurl each other around.

With raised umbrella and impressive blue-black necktie, this bird has plenty to display during courtship.

Golden Pheasant

"Pheasant" describes several species of brilliantly colored ground-living birds that are popular because they breed well in parks and large gardens. Golden pheasant males are particularly handsome, with their yellow-gold ruff and golden crest. Their mating display is a dance with head down, wings spread, and long tail raised in the air. A male performs singly to groups of three or four females, who are usually sufficiently impressed to mate with him.

Umbrella Bird

"Cravat bird" would better describe this male ornate umbrella bird. The "umbrella" is that crest of feathers over the eyes. More striking is the feather-covered wattle hanging from the throat like a cravat, or necktie. During courtship, males get together and dance from side to side, chattering and shaking their neckties.

Wood Duck

Wood ducks live along the borders of streams and in swampy forests. They nest in trees, often in the hollow trunks of willows and poplars. You find the nests 10 feet (3 m) or more above the ground, usually hidden in a hole in the trunk or deep among tangled branches. The female lines the nest with soft down and lays 6 to 12 eggs, which she incubates for about four weeks.

Raccoon

You see these little animals in many parts of the United States. They like to be in open country and close to water, where they can hunt for crayfish and insects. In colder regions, raccoons sleep during the winter, hiding in dens in hollow logs or burrows. In spring, when the time comes to start a family, pairs meet, mate, and build nests high in the trees. This family is snug and dry in a convenient hollow tree. Young raccoons emerge from the nest at about 12 weeks, and stay with their mother for almost a year before reaching independence.

• Hiding Away •

Hidden homes

At hatching, both parents stand below the nest, whistling. The ducklings leap one by one from the nest, parachuting down with feet spread and tiny wings flapping, adding their own shrill whistles to the chorus. Amazingly they land unhurt, and waddle off to the water with their parents.

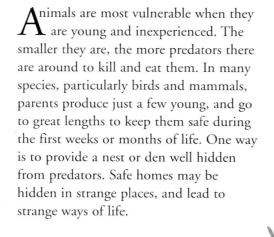

Animals are most vulnerable when they are young and inexperienced. The smaller they are, the more predators there are around to kill and eat them. In many species, particularly birds and mammals, parents produce just a few young, and go to great lengths to keep them safe during the first weeks or months of life. One way is to provide a nest or den well hidden from predators. Safe homes may be hidden in strange places, and lead to strange ways of life.

The wood ducks in the main picture are making a first appearance in the world. Hatched only a few hours ago in a treetop nest, they are parachuting down to join their parents in the water. Raccoons also nest high in the trees, in convenient hollows if they can find them. Incubating female hornbills imprison themselves in a hollow tree, while cloud swifts find safety for their nests behind the cascading spray of a waterfall.

Hornbill

Silvery-cheeked hornbills – two chicks and their mother – are imprisoned in a hollow tree in tropical Africa. Just before laying, the hen walled herself in, using a mixture of mud and saliva brought by her mate. She successfully incubated two eggs, while her mate brought her food. Imprisonment kept the family safe from predators.

Fledging at about eight weeks after hatching, the chicks break free from their mud-walled prison and take their first flight (above).

Cloud Swift

Sit by a waterfall in the rainforests of Brazil, and you may see dark shapes darting through the water. They are probably cloud swifts, feeding their chicks on the cliff face behind. It seems a strange place to raise a family, but swifts are remarkable birds, adapted more than almost any other kind of bird for life on the wing. Cloud swifts build tiny nests of moss on the cliffs behind a cascade. It may be damp and chilly, but it is safe. Few predators think of looking for them there.

A cloud swift (left) catches flying insects for its young, gathering and holding them in a pouch under the tongue.

Living underground

What safer place to make a home and protect young than under the ground? Burrows and underground dens reduce the chances of discovery by predators. They are cooler than the surface in summer and warmer in winter, and the limited number of entries and exits makes them readily defendable against unwelcome visitors. Burrows are especially useful for animals that live in large groups. In good soils there is plenty of space underground for them to excavate tunnels and chambers.

On these pages, the common earwig female is the homeowner with the smallest underground property – just a tiny cavity in the soil where she lays and defends her eggs. Timber wolf mothers find secret dens for their young, rearing them away from the pack until they are old enough to join. Rabbits, prairie dogs, and naked mole rats all create extensive underground warrens with passages and brood chambers, where they can live in relative safety from ground and aerial predators.

Rabbit

Rabbits probably originated in Europe but have spread with humans all over the world. One reason for their success is the care that mother rabbits (does) give to their young. Rabbits use their paws to dig burrows in the ground. An extensive group of burrows, perhaps several hundred dug over many years, is called a warren. Each doe has her own burrow; and within each burrow is a nesting chamber lined with grass and the doe's own fur. She defends her family fiercely against predators.

Rabbits nest in a burrow the doe can defend against predators.

Young wolves spend their first weeks in a den with their mother. When old enough to keep up, they run with the pack.

Timber Wolf

Timber, or gray, wolves spend most of their lives in packs of a dozen or more. In spring, pregnant females break away and dig dens for themselves, producing litters of 4 to 10 cubs. The mother tends her cubs in the den, feeding them first on milk, then on meat that she catches herself. At four to five weeks, they are old enough to join the pack.

Naked Mole Rat

These curious little rodents, naked except for scattered hairs, live in crowded underground colonies in the North African desert. On the surface, it is hot during the day and cold at night. Living underground gives them stable temperatures, and relative safety from eagles, hunting dogs, and other predators. Useful adaptations to underground living include tiny eyes and ears, and short legs and tails. Naked mole rats feed mainly on roots and bulbs. Only a few in each group get to breed, producing all the offspring for the colony.

Breeding females grow bigger than the others.

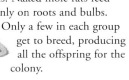

Non-working male

Worker, or non-breeder

Growing earwigs shed their skin twice before leaving the nest, and several times more before they become adults. Male earwigs have curved pincers, females' are straighter.

Male   *Female*

Common Earwig

There are about 900 different kinds of earwigs in different parts of the world. Nearly all live on damp ground, feeding on tiny animals and plant cells in the soil. They keep their family life secret, mating in tiny chambers and cavities within the soil, where the females also lay clutches of several dozen white eggs.

Unusual among insects, earwig mothers stay with and care for their eggs and young.

Females care for their eggs and nymphs in an underground nest, where they are well protected from weather and predators.

Prairie Dog

Prairie dogs live on North American grasslands in huge colonies called towns, often numbering thousands of burrows. Each town is divided into wards, and each ward is subdivided into smaller groups of burrows, with several entrances leading to a network of tunnels. Tunnel entrances are ringed by walls of earth up to 18 inches (45 cm) high, which keep floodwater out during rainstorms.

A nesting chamber (center) branches off a tunnel.

Tree Frog

This tree frog is one of several kinds that live in the damp tropical forests of Madagascar. Most frogs live in ponds, needing water close at hand for their eggs and tadpoles. In warm, rainy areas, trees become covered with mosses and other small plants, which soak up and hold moisture. There are even tiny ponds, way above ground, with enough moisture to keep frogs happy. Tree frogs, with flattened toes and fingers, climb rather than swim. Living among predatory birds, and lacking the poison of poison arrow frogs (pages 68–69), it pays them to match their backgrounds closely.

• Camouflage •
Matching the surroundings

Wild Pig

Domestic pigs, derived from wild pigs of Europe and Asia, are mostly pink, sometimes black or tan. Wild pigs have darker skins, and a darker and denser covering of hair, making them far less visible either in the forest or in open grassland. Domestic piglets, too, are uniformly pink. But wild ones like these are dark tan or brown, with white, yellow, or brown stripes, helping them hide from forest predators.

The word "camouflage" originally meant a wisp of smoke, blown in the face to deceive. In the animal world, camouflage is the trick by which animals come to match their background, often so well that they disappear completely from sight. Spot this tree frog among the green mosses and lichens, and you will appreciate how well it is camouflaged. Unless you knew it was there, looking very carefully, you might well miss it.

Camouflage affords protection against predators that hunt by sight, though less against those that hunt by sound or scent. It helps also to hide animals that are themselves predators, and lying in wait to catch others. Both kinds of animals appear on these pages. Common toads melt superbly into their surroundings. Such widely differing animals as elephant shrews and wild pigs are equally well camouflaged to match their different backgrounds. Sloths, slow and lazy as their name suggests, hide particularly well, going so far as to have green plants growing in their fur.

Checkered Elephant Shrew

Checkers is a game played on a board with alternate red and black squares. Checkered elephant shrews are small African mammals that take their name from the pattern of dark squares and rectangles in the paler fur along each side. These are obvious in the open, but make them almost invisible in undergrowth. They have other ways of disappearing, too. Long, thin legs, especially in the rear, give them an extraordinary ability to run and jump. If a hawk swoops down, they leap sideways and streak for home.

Common Toad

If you have a garden with cool, damp corners, you will almost certainly support a few resident toads. Small and squat, they live close to the soil, usually under stones or vegetation, for which their rough, bumpy, and mottled skin is a remarkably good match. A universal general-purpose camouflage, it clearly serves them well. You see little of them during the day. They come out mainly after dark, when they seek out and eat snails, slugs, and ants.

Sloth

"Sloth" is another name for laziness. Sloths live in the forests of South America, hanging upside-down from branches, grasping and munching leaves – perhaps spending their whole life in just one tree. They may lack ambition, but they are very good at camouflage. Their fur is the color of tree bark. Each hair is grooved, and green single-celled algae grow in the grooves, helping the sloth to match its background exactly.

Hiding

Camouflage is usually a visual trick, based on color or shape. It helps predators to hide from their prey, and prey to hide from predators. Species that cannot be hidden are often made to look like something else. Naturalists are astonished by the thousands of different ways in which camouflaging works, among a wide range of animals, from the simplest worms to the most complex reptiles, mammals, and birds.

"Now you see me, now you don't." In color, the bittern across the page almost exactly matches its background of reeds. See how it also hides by standing bolt upright with bill raised. If necessary, it will stay motionless for half an hour before relaxing and getting on with its business.

Shrimpfish have a similar trick of standing upright among anemone fronds. Frogmouths and marsupial numbats also remain very still when threatened, matching their backgrounds closely. Plaice move around, but within a few minutes change the colors in their skin to match their new backgrounds.

Shrimpfish

Shrimpfish hardly look like shrimps, but have a transparent bony covering like a shrimp's thin shell. Seen from the side, they are slender and tapering. Seen from below, they are almost transparent. When a shrimpfish stands upright in the water with its stomach toward you, it becomes almost invisible. This one has found a sea urchin with spines similar in color and shape to itself – almost perfect camouflage.

Numbat

This looks like a large, striped squirrel, but it is a numbat, a marsupial from the eucalyptus forests of southwestern Australia. Its main food is termites. The pattern of stripes blends wonderfully with the pattern of leaves and dappled sunlight on the forest floor. If frightened by a dog or other predator, the numbat runs and hides in a hollow log, blocking the entrance with its backside. The long nose hides a long row of teeth – 52 altogether, more than any other land mammal – and an even longer tongue.

Plaice

The seabed in coastal waters is full of life, and also full of danger. In searching for food, plaice alternately move and hide. Their skin contains sacs of paint-like pigments, which spread to show blobs of color, or contract to invisible pinpoints. In a few seconds the plaice can change color, matching its background wherever it lies.

Tawny Frogmouth

A dozen different species of frogmouths live in the forests of Asia and Australia. The huge bill that gives these birds their name is a trap for snapping up insects. The tawny frogmouth perches on a branch in a tree fork, close to moss and twiglets that match its feathers. Sitting very still and rigid, with eyes seemingly closed and bill pointing upward, it looks just like another branch. It is not quite so fast asleep as you might think, and the eyes are not completely closed. If you approach too close, it will wait till the last moment before flying away.

The frogmouth's enormous bill, with bright yellow lining, is said to attract the insects on which it feeds.

Bittern

You are more likely to hear bitterns than see them. They have surprisingly deep, booming voices that carry for miles across water. They live mainly near freshwater lakes, nesting among reeds by the water's edge. Now that many lakes have been filled in and built over, there are fewer bitterns around. If you hear one and want to see it, take a kayak and paddle along the edge of the lake. You'll need to look very closely to see a bittern in its alert posture, with its head pointing skyward, looking like a bunch of reeds. It is not lost in thought – those beady eyes will be watching you very closely.

Diamondback Rattlesnake

Western diamondback rattlesnakes live in desert areas of North America. Their name comes from the diamond shapes picked out along their backs. They hunt mainly at night, taking the small mammals and reptiles that emerge to feed after the heat of the day. During the day, they rest in whatever shade they can find. The snake's drab coloring matches the dry vegetation around it well. Now why should a well-camouflaged snake need a warning rattle? Simply to keep other animals – such as cattle, horses, and people – from blundering in and stepping on it accidentally.

• Camouflage •
Ready to pounce

Snowy Owl

Snow is white, but dappled gray and black with shadows. An entirely white bird would show up against a snowy background, whereas one like this snowy owl, with black streaks in its

plumage, blends in far better. In summer, an all-white bird would again become too obvious. One with streaked plumage blends better with the tundra and sky.

Camouflage helps animals to hide from danger, and is also an extra weapon for predators. Prey are easier to catch if they cannot see you. The rattlesnake opposite is dusty gray-brown, and covered with a pattern of diamonds. These help it disappear against the dusty desert background, where it lies in wait for the lizards and small mammals that are its prey. It is so well camouflaged that it needs an alarm – the rattle in its tail – to warn other, non-prey animals to avoid stepping on it by accident.

Arctic Fox and Hare

The Arctic, the region surrounding the North Pole, is snow covered for well over half the year. When the snow disappears in summer, the tundra landscape turns green and brown. Only a few animals, such as this arctic hare and arctic fox, live there all year round. Both benefit from being able to blend with their background. In the far north, they spend their winters in white coats, the fox bright to match the snow, the hare darker to match the shadows. In spring the foxes molt into brown furs, while the hares remain white.

Arctic foxes are white in winter, making them almost invisible against the snow, but brown in summer when their background is grass and rocks. Snowy owls are white with black streaks, a combination providing a measure of camouflage for all seasons. Crab spiders come in different colors. Programmed to find flowers of their own color, each ends up with a matching floral background, where it can sit and catch visiting insects.

The hare may be camouflaged, but so is the fox. Those that spot food first are first to survive in the harsh Arctic region.

Crab Spider

So called because it looks like a crab, this spider is one of several species that appear in a variety of colors. Their trick is to be able to find flowers of the same color as themselves. Pink crab spiders find appropriate pink flowers, blue ones blue flowers, and yellow ones yellow flowers. This yellow crab spider has done particularly well. It matches very closely the flower on which it sits – not only the petals, but the pollen, too. It matches so well that the wasp has failed to see it, and is about to be caught and killed.

A wasp is enticed into the trap.

• Glossary •

algae
Simple plants including many freshwater plants and seaweeds.

amphibians
Cold-blooded vertebrates, for example frogs and toads, that breed in water and live on land.

antennae
Sensitive feelers on the heads of crustaceans, insects, and other invertebrates.

camouflage
Use of colors or shapes to disguise an animal, hiding it from prey or predators.

carnivorous
Meat-eating.

caterpillar
Early stage in the life of a butterfly or moth.

chrysalis
Protective hard shell or casing enclosing the pupa or resting stage of a butterfly or moth.

cocoon
Protective case, spun from silky strands, enclosing the pupa or resting stage of an insect.

crustaceans
A large group of invertebrate animals, including crabs, lobsters, shrimps, and wood lice.

defense mechanism
A natural, self-protective reaction.

embryo
Early developmental stage of an animal, usually found within an egg or womb.

environment
The natural conditions in which plants and animals live.

fertilizing
Introducing male sperm into a female egg, producing embryos that grow into adults.

foraging
Searching for food.

incubating
Maintaining eggs at a constant warm temperature to insure their development.

invertebrates
Animals without backbones.

larva (plural, **larvae**)
Early stage in the development of many animals.

mammals
Warm-blooded vertebrates that bear their young alive and feed them on milk from mammary glands.

marsupials
Mammals that bear tiny young, keeping them in a pouch for the first few months of life.

microscopic
Tiny; visible only through a microscope.

migration
A regular, seasonal movement of a group of animals, such as caribou or terns, from one area to another.

nymph
Young form of an insect, such as a dragonfly or an earwig, that resembles the parent in some ways but is not yet mature.

parasite
Animal or plant that feeds only on other animals or plants.

predators
Animals that hunt other animals.

prey
Animals that are hunted.

pupa
Resting stage in the development of some insects, occurring between the larval and adult stages.

reptiles
Cold-blooded vertebrates, such as snakes, crocodiles, and lizards, that live mostly on land.

sea anemones
Soft-bodied marine animals with tentacles that open to look like flowers.

sociable
Living in a group.

species
Group of animals or plants (such as cows, blackbirds, or sunflowers) that are closely similar and able to breed with each other.

temperate regions
Regions of the earth that lie between tropical and polar regions.

tentacles
Long, thin feelers of invertebrate animals, used for touching and holding.

terrain
Ground on which plants or animals are living.

territory
Area of ground or sea defended by individuals or groups of animals for mating, nesting, roosting, or feeding.

tundra
Cold ground where trees cannot grow, found in Arctic and mountain regions.

venom
Poisonous fluid produced by snakes, scorpions, and other animals.

· Index ·